# Creating a
# Literacy Environment
# for Boys

## Ideas for Administrators,
## Teachers, and Parents

### CHRISTOPHER M. SPENCE

THOMSON

NELSON

Australia    Canada    Mexico    Singapore    Spain    United Kingdom    United States

Creating a Literacy Environment for Boys:
Ideas for Administrators, Teachers, and Parents
by Christopher M. Spence

**Director of Publishing**
Beverley Buxton

**Director of Literacy and Reference**
Joe Banel

**Executive Managing Editor,
Development**
Darleen Rotozinski

**Developmental Editor**
Jeff Siamon

**Editorial Assistant**
Lisa Peterson

**Executive Managing Editor,
Production**
Nicola Balfour

**Managing Editor, Production**
Karin Fediw

**Copyeditor**
Sandra Manley

**Index**
Noeline Bridge

**Production Coordinator**
Cathy Deak

**Design Director**
Ken Phipps

**Interior Design**
Peggy Rhodes

**Cover Design**
Ken Phipps

**Compositor**
Interactive Composition
Corporation

**Printer**
Transcontinental Printing

**COPYRIGHT © 2006** by Nelson, a division of Thomson Canada Limited.

ISBN-13: 978-0-17-628331-5
ISBN-10: 0-17-628331-5

Printed and bound in Canada
2  3  4  08  07  06

For more information contact Nelson, 1120 Birchmount Road, Toronto, Ontario, M1K 5G4. Or you can visit our Internet site at http://www.nelson.com

**Cover Image**
© James Noble/CORBIS

**Library and Archives Canada
Cataloguing in Publication**

Spence, Christopher Michael, 1962–
    Creating a literacy environment for boys: ideas for administrators, teachers, and parents / Chris Spence.

ISBN 0-17-628331-5

1. Boys—Books and reading.
2. Reading promotion. I. Title.

LB1050.5.S63 2005    028.5'341
C2005-904421-7

*To Jacob Robinson Spence*

# CONTENTS

# PREFACE

Jalen is a boy in grade 4. When asked what he thinks about people who read a lot, he says, "They need to get a life. I can think of more fun things to do than to just sit there." Ask him about reading, and he adds, "I don't like having to read for school. When I get to choose, it's all right, [but] I would only choose the good stuff."

When it comes to reading and writing, boys perform more poorly than girls all across Canada. Similar statistics can be found in over thirty other countries. In comparing boys and girls, boys

◆ say they are less committed to school

◆ don't read as many books

◆ are more likely to be held back in school, suspended from school, and drop out of school

◆ are three times more likely to be in special education classes

◆ are four times more likely to be diagnosed with attention deficit hyperactivity disorder (ADHD)

◆ are more successful in committing suicide, even though more girls make the attempt

(Heyman, 2003)

These are quite alarming facts.

But are boys really poor learners? Is there not something we, as educators and parents, can do to motivate more boys to become successful students? Does the disproportion of at-risk boys in the learning environment not say something about the way they are taught? Children, I believe, are natural learners. Given a chance, they will try to understand and use what we teach them.

So where have we gone wrong? Why does a boy like Jalen, who in every non-school aspect seems like a successful individual, feel that he's not getting "the good stuff" in school?

I was inspired to write this book by the birth of my son, Jacob. I want to give him opportunities to learn so that he can become a successful member of society. I want him to be part of a learning environment where being a boy isn't a disadvantage. I believe the school system needs to address how it is educating the young males of our society. There has certainly been enough research to show that boys and girls learn differently. At the same time, numerous studies have concluded that the school curriculum and many teachers do not take these gender learning and behavioural differences into account. What I offer to this discussion comes from my experiences as a teacher and administrator. I have taught, counselled, and mentored boys throughout my career. And, of course, I was a boy once myself.

My parents are from Jamaica, and I was born in England. There, soccer was my passion, and the sports pages were my and my brother's reading. Like so many young boys, we were more interested in becoming sports heroes than in being the teachers' favourites. I spent more time every evening reading the sports pages to my parents than I did with the books my teachers wanted me to read. My brother and I collected, organized, compared, and traded sports cards. No one ever told us that we were learning important literacy and numeracy skills.

When I was 8, my family moved to Canada. I discovered *Sports Illustrated* in the local library and became an avid reader. The magazine was the gift of choice for my brother and me. I also discovered that I was very good at playing soccer. The game brought meaning to my young life and gave me confidence to become successful academically and socially. Eventually, I earned an athletic scholarship to Simon Fraser University, starred as a running back on the football team, and received a degree in criminology. After graduation, I was drafted by the B.C. Lions of the Canadian Football League. When an injury ended my career three years later, I began working with young people in group homes and detention and treatment centres. These experiences eventually led me into teaching grade 6. I spent many of my teaching years in middle-school classrooms, and eventually became a principal and superintendent.

As a child, I was just a typical boy. I preferred physical activity to sitting and listening to adults. I wanted to read about real people doing real things instead of made-up stories about imaginary people. I wanted to be praised and accepted for who I was, not for who other people expected me to be.

From my work with young offenders to my years as a teacher, principal, superintendent, and now director of education, I have always had the desire to reach out to young people before they become failures in the school system. As educators, we have a moral purpose to make a difference in the lives of those we reach and teach. I know, from the important part reading played in my early years, that literacy is the key to success. I also know that like so many boys, I had to be physically motivated—not just intellectually stimulated—to learn.

As educators, we strive to ensure that every student has an equal opportunity to acquire learning skills and knowledge. We know from years of research the influence of gender learning styles and teaching methods—it's time to put this research into practice. Many boys learn differently from the majority of girls, especially in the area of literacy. Let's give these boys a chance to succeed.

## Acknowledgements

I would like to give a special note of thanks to the Boys to Men and Read to Succeed staff and students of the Hamilton-Wentworth District School Board and the Toronto District School Board. These outreach initiatives focus on helping boys develop the attitudes, skills, behaviours, and values necessary to perform at successful levels in school and society.

To my Friday night basketballers, thanks for keeping it real. B2M for life.

To my brother and sister, Everard and Jackie, and my parents, Sydney and Enez; I often think of the role you have played in my life. I can only feel gratitude for all you taught me to do, for all your words of encouragement, for what your lives gave me a chance to be.

To Joe Banel, Darleen Rotozinski, Sandra McTavish, and the Nelson Team for their unwavering support of this book from its beginning stages to its completion.

To Jeff Siamon, who, in addition to being the editor, helped considerably in the development stages of this book. His insights and critical review of the manuscript gave me the necessary encouragement to see the book through to its completion.

Finally, without the love, encouragement, and support of Marcia, Briana, and Jacob, this book would not exist.

# 1

# Five Top Reasons Why Boys Are Reluctant Readers

*"Students who can't read also give up. At first, they give up trying. Eventually, many of them give up on school. They sit in our classrooms disengaged, disinterested, and sometime defiant" (Beers 2003, 6).*

## Struggling and Reluctant Readers

Struggling and reluctant readers don't learn to read well for a variety of reasons, five of which are listed below. There are others: family background and attitude, poverty (an empty stomach doesn't fuel the brain), physical or mental disabilities, or simply missing school at a critical time. Regardless of the reasons, it is important to be able to recognize what makes

### Five Top Reasons Why Boys Are Reluctant Readers

- Biology influences how boys learn to read.
- There is not enough choice in what boys have to read in school.
- There are few male role models of good readers.
- Boys do not exhibit "good" classroom behaviour.
- Gender issues in the classroom disadvantage boys.

Figure 1.1

struggling readers remain reluctant. Teachers have no control over what goes on outside the school, but they can change the way reading is taught in the classroom.

How can you spot struggling and reluctant readers? They may

- sit in the back of the classroom or as far away from the teacher as they can get.
- disrupt the class during silent reading or when someone is speaking.
- get out of their seats when they are supposed to be reading silently.
- seem angry or upset—or simply refuse—when asked to read aloud.
- complain that all the reading material is "boring."

And, more than likely, many of these struggling readers are boys.

However, not all struggling readers are boys, nor are all girls excellent readers. Children with reading difficulties are individuals, and each fits somewhere on a continuum, from those who can't read at all to those whose reading levels are many grades higher than the norm. So it is important for educators to ask: Which boys and which girls have problems with reading? Otherwise, they run the risk of instituting one-size-fits-all classroom reforms that can create more problems than they solve.

During the 1970s and 1980s, there was a trend to ignore the differences between girls and boys. Educators believed that all children should be treated equally, and that they learn in the same way (Sommers 2000). However, we need to recognize that some boys learn differently from girls. More importantly, we need to understand why so many boys are unable or unwilling to become successfully literate in school.

## Biology Influences How Boys Learn to Read

Olga Silverstein, in *The Courage to Raise Good Men,* argues that the differences between boys and girls are culturally, not biologically, determined. "Though we may think it ageless and immutable, our conception of what constitutes the ideal man is cultural-bound" (Silverstein and Rashbaum 1994, 40). Silverstein argues that boys *learn* to be more restless in a classroom than girls, more delayed in language development and ability compared to girls, and more competitive and aggressive than girls. Society, she says, has created the strong, silent male and the weak, emotional female. Other educational researchers have questioned whether sex differences impede boys' literacy as much as family and societal influences: ". . . educators and parents can actively shape social worlds of youth and foster literacy development, rather than remain resigned to the notion that biology is destiny in literacy" (Gambell and Hunter 2000, 689–719).

"The neglect of gender in the raising and educating of children has resulted in a loss of direction for the growing child and especially the adolescent" (Sax 2005, 236).

However, recent research suggests that there are differences between boys and girls that are not caused by culturally inspired gender behaviour. They are, rather, "hard-wired" in children's brains. These biological differences can profoundly affect the way children learn to read and their chances of success in school.

### Brain Development

Research into the development of the human brain suggests that the brains of girls develop faster than boys' brains. Researcher Leonard Sax claims that "the brain of a 6-year-old boy looks like the brain of a 4-year-old girl; the brain of a 17-year-old boy looks like the brain of an 11-year-old girl; men don't catch up with women until they are 30 and in some areas [of brain develop-ment] they never catch up" (Sax 2001).

Research has also suggested that girls are more aware of the world around them than boys. They are able to take in and process "more sensory and emotive data, and more quickly than the male" (Gurian 1998, 183). It is little wonder that girls are better than some boys at figuring out the school system when they enter kindergarten and grade 1. They can see it, sense it, anticipate it. At the same age, many boys are just learning to share. Girls' brains not only develop faster, but girls also appear to use different areas of their brains than boys to do certain tasks, such as problem solving (Biddulph 1997, 58).

> "During the learning process, we often find girls using words *as they learn*, and boys often working silently. Even when we study student group process, we find females in a learning group using words more than males" (Gurian 2001, 45–46).

Brain development affects language acquisition. Although it is unwise to overgeneralize on research that is still ongoing, researchers have found that girls have more neural connections between the two sides of their brains and a better-developed left brain than boys. It is in the left side of the brain that language activity lies (ibid.).

Educators and parents do not need extensive research to see that many girls use and acquire language more fluently than many boys the same age. For example, hand a 4-year-old girl a car to play with and she can probably give it a name, imagine the car's personality, and invent a story for it. This activity is language-based, with the car serving as a language stimulator for words, emotions, and ideas. Give a 4-year-old boy a car and he will probably make car noises, and be more interested in its speed and direction than its personality.

Since boys are more right-brain oriented than girls, integrating spatial tasks with learning to read can help them develop

## Male and Female Brain Development

Here is a summary of what researchers now believe they have discovered about male and female brain development:

◆ Girls have stronger connections than boys among all the areas of the brain.

◆ The language centres in the brain develop earlier in girls.

◆ Boys have a more direct connection between their spinal cord and brain, allowing them to respond more quickly to physical danger.

◆ The area in the brain that controls speech is more active in girls.

◆ Boys and girls differ in how their brains process data and interpret sensory and bodily information.

◆ Girls appear to have a larger memory storage area in their brains.

(Kindlon and Thompson 2000, 31–33; Gurian 2001, 13–42; Haupt 2003; Heyman 2003, 7–9; Sax 2005, 11–39)

Figure 1.2

"good patterning and language" skills (Gurian 2001, 111–112). Curriculum documents that discuss the teaching of literacy skills to boys, such as *Me Read? No Way!*, acknowledge these skills by encouraging the use of "graphic organizers and other visual tools" as "a useful means of demonstrating the relationships between things, both spatially and conceptually" (Ontario Ministry of Education 2004(b), 19).

## Hearing

Girls are able to hear two to four times better than boys, depending on the frequency tested. This difference is present as early as children can be reliably tested (Cone-Wesson and Ramirez 1997; Cassidy and Ditty 2001).

Considering how young children hear can help a teacher create an equitable learning environment for both boys and girls. Perhaps, if boys have trouble hearing, they can take the front seats in classrooms. If students are grouped around tables, the teacher could walk around the room when speaking so that all children have the same chance of hearing what is said.

## Seeing

Picture a darkened classroom where a student is doing a presentation using overhead transparencies. Most of the girls are watching the screen with interest, but many of the boys are paying little attention. Are the boys unco-operative? Not necessarily. Researchers have discovered that females have better vision in dim rooms, whereas males see better in bright light (Gurian 2001, 30).

Because the retinas of boys and girls develop so differently, they see the world in different ways. Researcher Jennifer Connellan and associates at Cambridge University studied newborn babies to see if there were gender differences in what they preferred to look at. One hundred and two babies were videotaped on the day they were born. Next to each baby was a young, smiling woman and a mobile that moved. Neither the woman nor the mobile made any noise, and observers didn't know the sex of the newborn. The observations suggested that boy babies were more interested in the mobile, while girls were more likely to look at the smiling face, and that these reactions are biological, not behavioural (Baron-Cohen 2003).

Not surprisingly, these differences affect the performance and behaviour of school children. For example, because kindergarten boys are inclined to see the world in terms of things that move, they are likely "to simulate motion in their pictures" (Sax 2005, 21). Girls of the same age more often draw people, animals, and plants. "Psychologist Donna Tuman summarizes the difference [in the way boys and girls represent the world] this way: girls draw nouns, boys draw verbs" (ibid., 24). Boys often like dull colours such as black, grey, and blue; girls prefer the warm colours—red, orange, and yellow. Thus, when children draw, the boys' action scenes are dark and, especially at a kindergarten age, may appear as scribbling. The girls' faces and people are usually brightly coloured and symmetrical (ibid., 18–25). Without understanding the different ways boys and girls view and represent the world, it is easy to make faulty assumptions about their abilities and behaviour.

## Hormones

Boys and girls are neither biological machines, nor socialized stereotypical automatons. They are complex beings who are constantly changing and growing. One of the main factors for change is growth hormones: in the male, testosterone; in the female, estrogen and progesterone.

Most researchers agree that hormones have some effect on the way children behave in a group or class setting. When boys begin to experience levels of testosterone, they become more active. When these levels are high, they may do "better on spatial exams, like math tests, but worse on verbal tests" (Gurian 2001, 29). Competition can increase testosterone levels in both boys and girls, although boys' base levels are higher than those of girls. Thus, boys, on average, are often more competitive than girls, prefer group sports activities to individual ones, and are more inclined than girls to need to belong to a hierarchical peer group, especially in adolescence. Some of that behaviour can be attributed to male hormonal changes. Indeed, it has been found that when girls' testosterone levels increase, they also become more aggressive (ibid.).

## There Is Not Enough Choice in What Boys Have to Read in School

A three-year Prince Edward Island study of personal reading choices of students in grades 1 to 6 came up with some interesting statistics:

- Both boys and girls took out more fiction (60 percent) than nonfiction (40 percent) books from their school libraries.

- Girls checked out more library books than boys but not "in significantly different numbers."

- Boys took out about two-thirds of "all the information books . . . with less than one-third taken out by girls." (Doiron 2003)

"Students need the opportunity to select their own reading material at least as often as they read material selected by the teacher, and they need access to a wide variety of accessible materials. These are critical factors in ongoing reading achievement" (Ontario Ministry of Education 2003(c), 18).

Other researchers have found similar results (see Simpson 1996; Millard 1997; Smith and Wilhelm 2002). Gambell and Hunter concluded from their studies that "almost all the books read by girls were narrative fiction. In contrast, just over half of what the boys read were novels; nonfiction, comics, joke books and picture books comprised the remainder" (Gambell and Hunter 2000, 699).

Percentages aside, both boys and girls like to read fiction. However, in a 23-year study in England of the reading habits of 10- to 14-year-old children, researchers found that while the books boys and girls chose were similar in some categories (adventure, horror/ghost, animal-related, and crime/detective), there were many differences in the kinds of stories they chose. For example, boys favoured science fiction and fantasy twice as much as girls. Boys were four times less likely to choose romance/relationship stories and four times more likely to read sports-related books. In those categories that were similar, except for crime/detective, girls read "comparatively more" books than boys (Coles and Hall 2002).

Other researchers have found that magazines are the preferred reading material of all children with boys and girls again differing in their choices. Almost half the boys in one American survey read video game magazines as opposed to "seven percent of the girls surveyed" (Cox 2003). Boys also read more sports, computer, and music magazines than girls.

Canadian research has found results similar to British and American studies. Heather Blair and Kathy Sanford, in their three-year study conducted in western Canada, concluded that "boys are often disadvantaged in academic literacy as a result of current curricular emphases, teacher text and topic choices, and lack of availability and acceptability of texts that match [boys'] interests and needs" (2003). What boys read out of school is related to their personal interests such as "newspapers, sports magazines, computer magazines . . ., superhero comic books, and other graphic texts. These texts were a marked contrast to their in-school selections and were not seen as appropriate for in-school reading" (ibid.).

Much of what boys like to read is often not available in classrooms and school libraries: comics, sports, action and adventure magazines, fantasy, science fiction, and "blood and thunder" books (Millard 1997; Wilson 2005). Boys like to read about humorous incidents and bodily functions. They enjoy biographies of sports heroes and popular personalities. They like to read books with short chapters. But most interestingly, they want to read about things that are connected to the real world: how-to and informational books and magazines. In an Ontario school survey, "boys reported that they read a wide variety of materials outside of school, including newspapers (50%), comics (35%), manuals or instructions (25%), and magazines (64%). In addition, 82% of boys . . . wrote e-mail messages . . . " (Ontario Ministry of Education 2004(b), 7).

What is important to both boy and girl readers is *choice*.

As Hyatt and others have discovered, it is not necessarily true that boys do not read. Rather, "they do not like to read what they are presented with in the classroom" (Hyatt 2002). "Boys [in grades 3 and 4] generally [choose] books about sports, space, science, jokes and vehicles" (Doiron 2003). Perhaps in the interest of boys, teachers should follow Ron Jobe and Mary Dayton-Sakari's advice (2002, 13) for helping the struggling reader: "If you buy only one book for your classroom, choose the *Guinness Book of Records*!"

## There Are Few Male Role Models of Good Readers

Many researchers feel that more girls than boys are encouraged to read through adult modelling. As Scieszka points out (2002), "We tell boys that reading is important and that reading is for everyone; however, we show boys that reading is just for girls." When boys have predominantly female teachers—teachers who read to them, talk about reading, and encourage them to read—they assume that reading is essentially a female activity. In support of this notion, they also see mostly female school librarians. Boys are more likely to see their mothers reading than their fathers (Millard 1997, 83), and notice that it is the girls of their own age who are often avid readers.

William Pollack (1998, 147–149) has found that boys feel pressure not only to appear masculine, but also to not appear feminine. Some boys, particularly in adolescence, live in a narrowly defined world of masculinity in which everything they do or say is judged on the basis of the strength or weakness it represents. They think that it is "cool to be the fool," and that being "buddy-buddy with the teacher does not raise his stature in the eyes of his peers" (Sax 2005, 84–85).

As a teacher and administrator trying to engage boys in learning, I have had to deal with what Pollack has called the "boy code":

- ♦ "*The Sturdy Oak*—men should be stoic, stable, and independent . . . never show weakness."
- ♦ "*Give 'em Hell*—the stance . . . of extreme daring, bravado, and attraction to violence."
- ♦ "*The Big Wheel*—the need to achieve status, dominance, and power."
- ♦ "*No Sissy Stuff*—the gender straitjacket that prohibits boys from expressing feelings or urges seen (mistakenly) as feminine. . . . " (ibid., 24–25)

*Literacy for Learning: the Report of the Expert Panel on Literacy in Grades 4 to 6 in Ontario* concluded that students "need to see the connections between who they are, what they value, and what they are learning in school in order to make sense of the learning and integrate it into their whole being" (Ontario Ministry of Education 2004(a), 18). Children need to see connections in the real world between themselves and the activity of reading. They need to see their literacy connections in their teachers, peers, and parents who read. They need to see people at home as well as teachers and administrators—or visitors to the classroom such as local athletes—demonstrate their interest in reading. As Dorothy Strickland, Kathy Ganske, and Joanne Monroe point out (2002, 18), "Teachers who serve as inspiring models of reading and writing are passionate about their own literacy." Children deserve to see inspiring models, both male and female, who are passionate about reading.

## Boys Do Not Exhibit "Good" Classroom Behaviour

### Sit Still! Be Quiet!

I have encountered many examples in my teaching career that illustrate the notion that acting "cool" for children often means protesting against school and schoolwork. This behaviour cannot merely be explained by biology or societal expectations. Educators have to look at what children bring to a classroom and what the classroom offers them.

As Gambell and Hunter and others have found in their research, "boys arrive at school as active, aggressive and independent, but must adjust to a school environment that values quietness, passivity and conformity. When teachers are not able to meet males' need for attention, boys go from calling out to acting out, adopting a bad boy role . . ." (Gambell and Hunter 2000, 696).

This is what the average educational environment asks of children in class:

- that they raise their hands if they have a question and *sit still and be quiet* for the answer
- that they refrain from roughhousing and aggressive competition—and *sit still and be quiet*
- that they curb their desire to move around and talk during class lessons—and *sit still and be quiet*
- that if they will only *sit still and be quiet,* they can stay out of trouble

Every student is expected to sit still to listen, to read, to solve problems, and to do schoolwork independently or in groups. Unfortunately, for many boys, sitting still is not a normal phenomenon.

### Bad Boys, Good Girls

In my experience, boys are usually physical and emotionally transparent, and sometimes enjoy being "bad." I only needed to be absent from my middle-school classroom for one day to get proof of this behaviour. I would come back to horror stories of how bad the boys had been. It was as if they could not control themselves and took great pleasure in making the substitute teacher's day miserable. The girls were also taking advantage of my absence. They were quietly going against the substitute's wishes by ignoring instructions they didn't want to follow or by setting the classroom agenda. The difference was *how* the boys and girls were bad. The girls' behaviour was much more subtle, less physical and boisterous, and thus perceived as "good," that is, acceptable.

"By school age, the average boy in a classroom is more active than about three-fourths of the girls, and the most active children in the class are very likely to be boys. And even the more active girls don't seem to express their energy in the unrestrained way more characteristic of boys" (Kindlon and Thompson 2000, 32).

Boys are more likely than girls to engage in disruptive behaviour and be off-task (Gambell and Hunter 2000). Boys do get more attention than girls in the classroom, but these interactions come about because of discipline and class management issues. Children need incentives to be successful at school. They need to interact in a positive way with their teachers and the other students. When their interactions are more often negative, the wrong type of behaviour gets reinforced.

## Gender Issues in the Classroom Disadvantage Boys

### One Size Fits All?

Treating boys and girls equally in the classroom has probably been contentious since the beginning of co-educational school systems. In the past, "hard" subjects, such as the physical sciences, math, and those requiring strength and manual dexterity, were commonly considered male subjects. "Soft" subjects—often language-based—such as English, social studies, and sciences without a heavy math foundation, were considered female subjects. This educational culture was comfortable in pre-determining both what boys and girls should learn and what they should be good at learning.

I would certainly not advocate returning to that model of education! However, boys and girls do learn differently. These differences exist despite the fact that some "teachers do not want an individualistic child. . . . They want a collective. They want everybody to be that one model student . . ."

> "Many British educational leaders believe that the modern classroom fails boys by being too unstructured, too permissive, and too hostile to the spirit of competition that so often provides boys with the incentive to learn and excel" (Sommers 2000, 160).

(Smith and Wilhelm 2002, 100). But many boys don't fit this profile of a model student.

Research has shown that boys typically like competition and thrive on it, while girls are more co-operative. Many boys respond well to a classroom environment that is active and structured. They benefit from small-group instruction, clear expectations, and behavioural limits. They need frequent changes in activities and opportunities to burn off excess energy. While some girls also fit this pattern, many are more able to work independently. Many girls participate successfully in small-group discussions, are more self-directed, have little difficulty with open-ended tasks and expectations, and are more able than boys to sit and concentrate for long periods of time (Sommers 2000; Heyman 2003, 7–9).

Because boys are often more task oriented than many girls, they like to problem solve—they like to know what the problem is and then get on with solving it. Girls are interested in solving problems, too, but go about it differently: they are more likely to begin by talking about the issue, and entertain the possibility that there might be more than one solution. Neither approach is better or worse, just different—the way boys and girls are different.

## The Change in Teacher Demographics

Why don't boys like to read in school? As Hyatt noted (2002), "None of the boys had a dislike for literacy. They only rejected school literacy." And what is wrong with "school literacy"? Perhaps part of the answer lies in the changing proportion of male and female teachers in the last few decades. Once, students in middle schools and high schools encountered primarily male teaching staff. Now, not only in the early grades, but in high school as well, they find mostly female teachers.

Many educators recognize that the imbalance of male and female teachers has inadvertently created a learning culture where the male voice is seldom heard. There is research that connects the decline in literacy of male students with the decline in the number of male educators (Ontario College of Teachers 2004; Bernard, Hill, and Falter 2004, 5). For example:

♦ In the Ontario Grades 3 and 6 Assessments of Reading, Writing, and Mathematics for 2003–2004, a larger percentage of girls than boys performed at or above the grades 3 and 6 provincial standards in reading, writing, and mathematics. In grade 3 reading, 59 percent of girls and 48 percent of boys performed at or above the provincial standard. In both grades 3 and 6 reading, twice as many girls achieved level 4 as boys. As well, more boys than girls were assessed at levels 1 and 2 (EQAO 2004).

♦ Boys entering school in Canada made up about 50 percent of the school population in 1999–2000, but 10 percent more females graduated high school than did males. In 1999, boys were nearly one and a half times more likely to leave school before graduation than girls (Canadian Education Statistics Council 2003).

◆ In the ten years from 1989/1990 to 1999/2000, census data shows that the percentage of full-time male educators in Canada dropped from 41 percent of the workforce to 35 percent. The percentage of young male educators was even lower, accounting for just 22 percent of educators aged 20 to 29. With 40 percent of male educators aged 50 years or older in 2000, and the lower rate of males entering the profession, female educators may soon outnumber their male co-workers by as much as four to one (Canadian Education Statistics Council 2003; Jamieson 2005).

These trends are not just restricted to Canada. Similar statistics can be found in the United States and around the world. In a 2001 survey of the fifteen countries of the European Union, for example, significantly more females than males were in school by the age of 18. In England, the rate was nearly 10 percent higher for girls. In Ireland, the difference was as great as 27 percent more girls than boys in school at age 18. For twenty-one of the twenty-nine countries surveyed by UNESCO, women accounted for 60 percent of all educators (Dunne 2003). In Canada, the rate is about 65 percent.

◆ "The low number of male teachers constitutes a growing challenge to the teaching profession in Ontario and raises important questions around the balance of education provided to the province's boys and girls, young women and young men" (Ontario College of Teachers 2004).

The increasing proportion of female educators has created an educational culture that affects the school environment—from the physical set-up of the classroom to the way subjects are taught. There is an increasing emphasis on co-operation instead

> "Creating an environment in middle and high school where literacy flourishes means making classrooms physically, academically, and psychologically safe for learning. Students must believe that they are significant members of a community of learners. . . . When students trust their teacher and their classmates, even weaker students will take risks to read, write, ask questions, and participate" (Taylor and Collins 2003, 62–63).

of competition and on an open-ended, discussion-based teaching and learning style. These approaches to education have value. Boys as well as girls need to work co-operatively. They need to develop their ability to think laterally. They need to be able to work for extended periods of time on a single task until it is successfully completed. And they also need a learning environment that gives each student—male or female—a fair chance of learning these skills. Not all styles of learning are necessarily natural to all types of students.

## Overcoming the Roadblocks to Literacy

Schools can be one of the main engines of social change. They can set the tone of society in ways no other institution can match. They can transform boys and girls into children who are caring, thoughtful, and intellectual. However, the academic and societal challenges that confront boys in school settings suggest an urgent need for thoughtful intervention. We need initiatives that will help boys develop the skills, behaviours, and values necessary to perform at optimal levels in school and society.

Regrettably, I have found that more boys than girls believe school to be a waste of time. Educators must take note of why boys feel this way. They also must approach teaching literacy and subjects that are language-based in a way that suits both boys and girls. I realize that the answers to the question "Why do boys have trouble with literacy?" and the solutions are not simple. But there are a number of approaches educators can take:

♦ Develop a multifaceted, comprehensive approach to the education of both boys and girls by acknowledging gender differences.

♦ Move beyond a "tips for teachers" approach and merge research-based knowledge with a comprehensive and thorough understanding of how boys and girls learn.

♦ Use research data—not stereotypes—to analyze how gender differences along with other factors affect educational outcomes.

♦ Develop an understanding of curriculum subjects that relates to student development.

♦ Identify and critically reflect on the best teaching practices. Align high-quality teaching practices with assessment methods and curriculum initiatives.

♦ Encourage ongoing, substantive, professional conversations and professional development.

♦ Ensure that strategies such as peer support, mentoring, cross-age tutoring, and buddy reading programs are developed in learning environments.

♦ Evaluate both the academic and social outcomes of programs or strategies.

♦ Nurture positive relationships among boys, girls, and adults of both sexes.

♦ On top of all that, celebrate the individual!

Although there are many difficulties facing educators as they try to encourage boys to become better readers, I hope to show that these challenges are not insurmountable.

# 2

# Research-Based Knowledge

*"Information is the starting point for improving student achievement. A wide range of information helps educators to see what is and is not working in classrooms and at the school and board levels, and points the way to changes that will reduce the gap between high- and low-performing students while maintaining high standards for all students"* (Ontario Ministry of Education 2004(b), 29).

Marva Collins taught in the inner-city Chicago public school system in the 1970s and 1980s. After fourteen years of frustration, she decided to start her own school. Her success in teaching poor, urban children is based on the assumption that *all children can learn.* She maintained that "if a student didn't learn it, then I didn't teach it" (Collins 1992, 9). This statement is a challenge for teachers who are asked to deal with changing curriculums, split grades, and classes of up to thirty-five students whose reading abilities range from two grades below the standard to several grades above. As shown earlier, there are many factors that make it difficult for some children, particularly boys, to learn.

What Collins and others have come to realize is that teachers need a wide range of knowledge about their students. This information is based on systematic research or what is called *research-based knowledge.*

Teaching begins with the student. Knowing him or her is fundamental to using successful teaching practices. Any success

Research-Based Knowledge 29

## Research-Based Knowledge

Below are four basic steps or practices that I follow when doing research-based knowledge.

### Data Collection

◆ Researching the learning environment.

◆ Finding out who the students are: their backgrounds, their abilities, their stages of cognitive and physical development, and their attitudes.

### Evaluation

◆ Evaluating the collected data in order to develop effective teaching strategies suited to the diversity of the students.

◆ Seeking support for these evaluations from other teachers, consultants, principals, board of education administrators, parents, and volunteers in the community.

◆ Becoming a leader of and champion to the students, especially to those who have been unsuccessful learners.

### Intervention

◆ Applying what has been learned about the students by putting into practice effective teaching strategies.

◆ Using a variety of resource people to help implement the strategies.

### Re-assessment

◆ Re-evaluating the learning goals and teaching strategies according to the students' performances.

◆ Being aware that this approach to teaching is an iterative process. If students still are having difficulty learning, assumptions need to change and the process begun again.

Figure 2.1

that I have had as a teacher and administrator has come about because I have tried to incorporate research-based knowledge into my teaching practices.

Most teachers use some form of research-based knowledge. It is not the methodology, however, that is effective, so much as the systematic manner in which it is applied. It is important to gather information about students *before* planning lessons and teaching strategies. For example, doing a social studies unit that is exclusively language-based will not suit a class of students who are having difficulty reading.

"Careful examination of *individual* student data will help ensure informed decision making about the effectiveness of current policies and which specific *groups* of students your literacy system should target and measure" (Taylor and Collins 2003, 20).

Basing an evaluation on another teacher's anecdotal comments or the student's previous year's work does not take into account that the student might have matured in the interim. As I often tell teachers when confronted with a misbehaving student, think before taking action: "Whatever your first reaction is, *do not do it*!" We need to set aside our prejudgments and assumptions when encountering a new group of learners or a new learning situation for a familiar student.

## Turning Data into Knowledge

Collecting student data beyond standard classroom assessments (e.g., assignments and tests) can be very time-consuming. It needs to be a school-wide practice that is ongoing throughout the school year. It requires planning and a team approach, from the classroom to the school to the board of education. Thus, schools and boards of education need to consider

1. developing a school- or board-wide plan to acquire qualitative and quantitative student data.

2. focusing on a process for examining and analyzing this data.

3. initiating a system for disseminating research results.

4. ensuring that materials are available to support the teaching practices.

Figure 2.2

## A Model for Research-Based Knowledge

### Characteristics of Boy Students

Some characteristics of boy students for the three areas of development are listed in Figure 2.3 on the next page (Piaget 1976; Labinowicz 1980). Many of these characteristics have been discussed in some detail in Chapter 1.

"There is so much pressure today for accountability in the schools that some educators immediately get defensive when they hear the word 'assessment'" (Taylor and Collins 2003, 49).

These observations are generalities. To understand how they might apply to specific students, educators need to gather and analyze their own data.

The research model used here is based upon interviews and observations of boy students. This anecdotal information is then

## Characteristics of Boy Students

| Cognitive | Physical | Social/Emotional |
| --- | --- | --- |
| ◆ deductive reasoners | ◆ often active rather than passive | ◆ not inclined to ask for help |
| ◆ good at spatial relationships | ◆ poorer hearing and vision than girls | ◆ sometimes underestimate reading ability |
| ◆ task oriented, yet may have poor attention span | ◆ better at physical tasks than verbal ones | ◆ generally don't have a strong need to please adults |
| ◆ sometimes delayed in language development | | ◆ peer group very important |
| | | ◆ often not aware of own feelings |
| | | ◆ communication not always a strength |

Figure 2.3

organized around the three developmental areas. Inferences and implications are made from the data, along with a summary of what has been learned about the student. The model concludes with a discussion of where the student is developmentally, his strengths and weaknesses, and the type of learning environment and teaching strategies that best suits the student's needs.

| Knowledge-Based Research Record Sheet |
| --- |
| Name: |
| Pre-assessment: |
| Area of Development: |
| Inferences: |
| Implications: |
| Summary: |
| Conclusion: |

Figure 2.4

## The Model—Pre-Assessment

Arnold is a ten-year-old boy in grade 5. He is the only child in a two-parent family. The following is part of the first formal interview I did with the boy.

| | |
| --- | --- |
| *Teacher:* | *Arnold, what do you like most about school?* |
| Arnold: | (after a pause and a big grin) I like everything—all my friends are here. . . . Recess is fun. |
| *Teacher:* | *What makes it fun?* |
| Arnold: | I can eat and play with friends. |
| *Teacher:* | *Do you have a favourite subject?* |
| Arnold: | Well, not really. I like all my subjects, but French is pretty good because I get to do stuff with my friends. |
| *Teacher:* | *How do you mean?* |
| Arnold: | We work in groups to get the work done, then we have no homework. |
| *Teacher:* | *So you like working in groups?* |
| Arnold: | Yeah, it's easier because everyone in our group is smart, then we don't have to do homework. |
| *Teacher:* | *Do you learn a lot from your friends?* |

| | |
|---|---|
| Arnold: | Yeah, I guess so. We get the work done fast, and then we talk about anything and crack jokes. |
| Teacher: | *What do you talk about?* |
| Arnold: | Umm . . . I don't know, all kinds of stuff—like Rapinder was telling us why he can't go out for Halloween 'cause we were talking about costumes. |
| Teacher: | *Do you talk about school stuff?* |
| Arnold: | Uhh . . . sometimes if we have a test or something. |
| Teacher: | *Arnold, thanks for talking with me. I know you want to get outside for recess.* |
| Arnold: | Yup. Bye. |

"Boys succeed when they know that their reading and writing—and their progress as readers and writers—are valued. Responsive, high-quality assessment at various stages of a student's work and clear feedback, including both recognition for good work and clear guidance on how to improve, are important to all students. For boys, however, assessments based on clear criteria and specific and immediate feedback are crucial" (Ontario Ministry of Education 2004(b), 43).

This interview with Arnold made me realize just how important group interaction and socialization is to him. Children—specifically boys—in this age group are becoming more sociocentric and are very interested in the views of others. Arnold learned from his friend Rapinder why he is not allowed out at Halloween. The learning that took place in that discussion will foster respect for ethnic differences and a capacity for critical literacy when Arnold is exposed to written text and other media.

## The Model—Cognitive Development

### Observations

**September 27:** *Observing Arnold with a math assignment.* The children have been asked to find the sum of two numbers and put them in order from smallest to largest. Arnold looks over the assignment and grins at his neighbour. He then remarks, "This is easy."

**September 27:** *Observing Arnold in a social studies class.* The lesson is on latitude and longitude and using maps. Arnold hasn't reviewed the assignment, but talks to his neighbour instead. The two laugh. The teacher asks Arnold to "get to work" on two occasions, and Arnold begins to work both times. When he begins to work on the assignment, he is out of his seat to ask the teacher for assistance. As he works, his face expresses puzzlement.

**October 4:** *Observing Arnold reading his "monster for a day" story to the class.* He pronounces words and sentences properly. His use of pronouns and sentence structure is appropriate. The other students enjoyed the story as evidenced by their laughter. The vocabulary and content he uses are standard for grade 5, and he is able to use phrases and clauses satisfactorily.

### Inferences

When considering these observations, my initial reaction is that Arnold was just being disruptive and was not focused on the assignments. However, Arnold's difficulties in social studies may be related to his inability to deal with the complexities of scaling and the abstractions of longitude and latitude (Piaget 1976; Labinowicz 1980). (He was not the only student having difficulty with this assignment.) Arnold is also at an age where his self-confidence is emerging (Norris and Boucher 1980). His oral language appears to be standard for his age. He uses humour to maintain his self-confidence and build the cohesiveness of the group. He is able to proofread and is concerned with using proper punctuation and spelling. He can read with rhythm and convey an understanding of mood, plot, setting, and characterization—all of which are age appropriate (ibid.) and important to developing critical literacy.

## Implications

Arnold's inattention and clowning around are indicators of his level of thinking. His teacher, however, should refrain from making snap assumptions—namely that Arnold is just being bad. Possibly, he is not paying attention or co-operating for a number other reasons:

♦ He is afraid he cannot meet the teacher's expectations.

♦ He is afraid he is not able to do the assignment.

♦ He does not understand the assignment or the teacher's expectations.

♦ Or—in a worst-case scenario—all of the above reasons.

Teachers need to be observers before introducing new concepts, ensuring that students have the necessary intellectual capabilities to learn the subject. For example, children in the concrete operational stage (Piaget 1976; Labinowicz 1980) can complete the following addition: $6 + 1 = 7$. They can also explain that seven is an odd number. But to assume they understand that adding one to any even number will always make the answer odd is likely expecting too much of them.

## Summary

Arnold is comfortable with concrete tasks and clear expectations. He understands basic abstract symbols when they can be associated with something concrete that he understands. To use Piaget's stages of cognitive development as a model, Arnold is at a "concrete operational stage" (Piaget 1976; Labinowicz 1980). He is not ready to make inferences about concepts that have no real connections to his concrete world. For example, he can apply number symbols to real objects, but longitudinal and meridian lines are pure abstractions, and he cannot picture them. The teacher needs to find concrete "hooks" for these and other abstract ideas in order to help Arnold make the connections.

## The Model—Physical Development

### Observations

**September 27:** *Arnold is in gym class.* He does not bring appropriate gym attire to the class. He sits on the stage and will not participate. The teacher responds to Arnold's behaviour by saying that today he will participate in gym wearing his street clothes.

**October 4:** *Arnold is in gym class.* He is working with a group of four students on soccer skills (i.e., heading, trapping, and passing). He is fluid and coordinated and is able to judge the speed and direction of the soccer ball as it approaches him. He is able to hit the ball with his head, as well as trap and pass it.

**October 11:** *Arnold is in gym class.* He comes into the gym and is constantly moving around. His actions and movements appear to be unrelated to any specific task.

### Inferences

Arnold's ability to coordinate his eye/head and foot/ball movements is appropriate for his age (Norris and Boucher 1980, 11). I thought his reluctance to participate might be because he has difficulty with his soccer skills, but his fluidity and coordination

does not support this idea. Perhaps he does not want to participate because he thinks his soccer skills are just at or below
average. I learn that before September 27, he has repeatedly
forgotten his gym clothes during this soccer unit. Each time he
has forgotten them, he has not had to participate, reinforcing
the notion: no clothes, no soccer practice.

At first, I believed Arnold's actions were just a sign that he
was abnormally active. But researching the physical developmental stages for boys his age suggests that his high energy level
is normal (ibid.).

## Implications

Arnold excels in cross-country activities. He never forgets his
gym clothes. Soccer is different because there are more students
participating and many are quite good at the sport. Arnold is
taller and more physically developed than the other boys, but he
is not as athletic. He needs a sports environment that does not
stress competition. This would help reduce the anxiety he feels
that he has to be the best at everything. Perhaps as a follow-up to
assessment, Arnold can be introduced to books such as *Leo the
Late Bloomer* by Robert Kraus and Jose Aruego which could
provide opportunities to discuss his anxieties.

## Summary

Arnold is the kind of child who puts high expectations on himself
and can be easily frustrated. He wants to be the best, fastest,
strongest, and most skilful in the class and feels threatened by the
skills of others. Because of his size, the children in the class assume
he is a good athlete. In a small group, Arnold feels comfortable and
relaxed after he gets over his initial avoidance technique. However,
when the class comes together for a competitive game, Arnold is
hesitant to participate, as his soccer skills would be evaluated by
his peers, and his team would be expected to win. When he does

eventually participate, he does quite well as his competitive spirit, which is characteristic of this age group, comes out (ibid., 9–11). It is normal for children to feel the pressure of competition. While it can be a powerful motivator for boys of his age, if boys like Arnold feel that the stakes are too high, they meet the challenge by avoidance.

## The Model—Social/Emotional

### Observations

**October 11:** *Arnold works co-operatively with a group of four students.* They are given one atlas and one handout with questions. Arnold takes both and puts them in front of himself. He says something that makes the rest of the group laugh. He opens the atlas to get the group started on the assignment.

**October 11:** *Arnold plays a computer game with one of the other students.* They are outside, laughing and enjoying themselves as they take turns playing the game. Arnold remarks that the game is just like the one he has at home.

**October 18:** *Arnold shows his completed work to the teacher.* He is all smiles as they talk about the assignment.

### Inferences

The emergence of leadership and the anxiety to win are characteristics of this age group (ibid.). Arnold is clearly the leader of the group. I make this inference because he takes control of the atlas and handout by putting them in front of himself. He is the one that gets the group started on the assignment even though he is constantly looking around at the other groups. Theorist Rudolf Dreikurs (Dreikurs, Grunwald, and Pepper 1982) suggests that only children are much more social than children with siblings. Arnold's day-to-day interactions with other children seem to support this observation. He is constantly telling jokes or seeking peer approval.

I thought Arnold might have some difficulty sharing the computer game, because only children typically tend to be self-centred. However, Arnold is co-operative and willing to understand the points of view of others. Arnold's comment that the game is just like the one he has at home may seem slight, but it exemplifies his stage of development. He is able to think about physically-absent things that are based on past experiences (Piaget 1976; Labinowicz 1980).

## Implications

For children like Arnold, it is important not to underestimate the influence of peers. Thus, I would suggest a learning environment that promotes co-operation. Arnold loves to work with his peers and learn from them. It is a good idea to capitalize on these strengths.

## Summary

When observing Arnold with his peers, I anticipated some difficulties because Arnold is an only child. Only children spend their childhood among those that are more proficient. I thought Arnold would devote much of his energy trying to get teacher approval. However, Arnold was much more interested in peer acceptance, even though some only children are egocentric. Theorist Rudolf Dreikurs suggests that only children are much more social than children with siblings (Dreikurs, Grunwald, and Pepper 1982). Arnold has emerged as a leader in the group and continues to thrive on socialization. I feel that he looks forward to coming to school because of the socializing.

## The Model—Conclusion

Arnold is able to think logically and systematically about concrete objects and concepts. Therefore, he had no difficulty in finding the sum of two numbers and putting them in order from smallest to largest. However, he did have problems understanding the complexities of scaling and the abstractions of longitude and latitude. His intellectual ability allows him to understand only some mathematical and scientific concepts, generally those that are connected to his real world.

One of Arnold's strengths is his ease and ability to speak in front of a group. He likes being the centre of attention and thrives on being a leader. Like many boys his age, Arnold learns best when he is active. He needs to be able to move around the class while he is engaged in a lesson. He is also a good reader and is careful about the correctness of his writing.

Because he needs concrete materials to help him in his learning, I suggest a learning environment where there are manipulatives for him to use. As well, his teacher should take advantage of his leadership skills by giving him tasks that he is responsible for completing. For example, in a social studies class I had with Arnold, I asked him to be the Thermometer Monitor. His task was to go outside for twenty minutes with the thermometer, observe the temperature, and then share his observations with the class. When he reported to the class, he had a happy glow on his face the whole time he had the class's attention.

There are two other teaching suggestions I would make to encourage Arnold in his learning—these because he is so sociocentric:

♦ **Thought Book**—Each morning when the children come into class, they write or sketch what is on their minds. At the end of the week, they share with the class what they have recorded in their Thought Books. Arnold is confident when expressing himself in print or orally. Here would be a non-competitive opportunity for him in which to be successful.

♦ **Drama**—In large group situations, Arnold becomes easily distracted if he feels anxious about competing. However, he is good at co-operating with others when clear goals have been established such as those associated with doing drama: memorizing a play script, following the directions, making the set and costumes, and so on.

What I learned about Arnold is that he is a natural leader and more social than many boys his age. These qualities in the wrong class setting could be construed as misbehaving. In a learning environment that is co-operative, gives children opportunities to move around, and encourages social inter-action, Arnold's apparent weaknesses will become his strengths. In a typical classroom setting, these strengths might go unrecog-nized without the insights that come from research-based knowledge.

# 3

# Instructional Leadership in the Classroom

> "If you have lots of boys in an English or language arts class—or so the conventional wisdom goes—you can expect to have problems. We've been fascinated to see teachers who would never link a troubled classroom to their students' racial, ethnic, or social class background feel comfortable linking the problems to the relative proportion of boys and girls. It seems that gender is a category that teachers use to think with" (Smith and Wilhelm 2002).

## Listening to What Boys Have to Say

Boys who struggle with reading often struggle with feelings of inadequacy and powerlessness. They feel disconnected from the classroom learning culture. As Smith and Wilhelm reported in their research (2002, 20), a majority of boys felt that "teachers need to do a better job at caring about them as individuals." Teachers can do "a better job" if they listen to what the boys have to say about the school environment. For example, boys—when pressed for a definition of "reading"—will probably say that it is an activity done in school, and they are likely to describe themselves as non-readers. Yet boys read CD covers and liner notes, video-game manuals, magazines not in the school library, retail catalogues, newspapers, road and store signs, sports cards, e-mail messages, instructional books and articles, and product information. In fact, most boys read all the time, but they do not associate these activities with what many school literacy programs define as "reading." In the past, schools' ideas of literacy placed the focus on literature-based reading curriculums that did not include CD covers and the like. More recent curriculum documents such as Ontario's *Literacy for Learning* (Ontario Ministry of Education 2004(a)) recognize a more inclusive literacy.

> "Understanding that texts exist in many forms helps students and teachers to apply literacy learning to the wider world, and leads to deeper thinking and more effective communication" (Smith and Wilhelm 2002, 6).

## What Boys Think About Reading

Patrick Jones and Dawn Cartwright (2003) found that boys identified the following reasons why they do not read:

| Rank | Reason | Percent of Boys |
|------|--------|-----------------|
| | **What Boys Think About Reading** | |
| 1 | Boring, not fun | 39.3 |
| 2 | No time or too busy | 29.8 |
| 3 | Like other activities better | 11.1 |
| 4 | Can't get "into" the stories | 7.7 |
| 5 | Not good at reading | 4.3 |
| 6 | Become tired and/or get headaches | 2.5 |
| 7 | Video games and/or TV more interesting | 2.3 |
| 8 | Too much schoolwork to do | 1.4 |
| 9 | Books are too long | 0.09 |
| 10 | Ridicule from friends | 0.01 |

Figure 3.1

If research shows that boys think reading is boring and do not have the time for it, educators need to re-evaluate how reading is taught. This re-evaluation is a multi-step process. Teachers can begin by

♦ *researching the learning styles of boys and girls.* As chapter 1 illustrated, many boys learn differently from girls. Teachers should approach literacy instruction with these differences in mind.

♦ *introducing into their classrooms a more active and visual style of learning.* Teachers should include drama, visual-art displays, debates, and design projects that require reading and writing.

♦ *developing reading activities that better match what boys really read.* Teachers need to bring into the classroom reading materials that boys read, proving to boys that what they value as reading, teachers also value.

Educators also need to understand that boys perceive their school behaviour differently from their teachers. These perceptions can affect their learning performance (Pollack 1998, 227; Smith and Wilhelm 2002, 10). For example, boys may ask themselves: *Why work harder when I'm already doing all right?* (Pollack 1998, 237–238; Sax 2005, 113) They might hide learning difficulties behind behavioural problems: *Why not clown around when the teacher asks me a question?* They might assume that their teachers expect less of them than they do the girls in their classes: *Why do my schoolwork when I can never be the top student?* (Sommers 2000, 33–38) Educators need to change these perceptions if they are going to be successful in improving boy literacy.

## Lesson Planning for Boy Learners

The strategies that teachers use to teach reading should be developed out of what their research has told them about their boy students. With this information in mind, teachers need to

◆ observe boys as they read to determine their strengths and weaknesses.

◆ use this knowledge to help choose appropriate reading strategies.

◆ devote instructional time to showing boys how to use and evaluate reading strategies.

◆ provide boys with opportunities to practice the strategies they have been taught.

◆ present reading strategies across the curriculum and in a variety of school and non-school contexts to reinforce the idea that reading can be done outside of the language arts class.

◆ model being active readers themselves by reading in class and participating in discussions.

"When students learn to learn in more meaningful ways, they are more likely to develop intrinsic motivation for learning rather than being solely focused on tests and grades for credentials" (McKeachie 1995).

The instructional goal is to work toward a learning environment where boys feel responsible for their own learning. In an ideal classroom, teachers become the facilitators and boys are their own teachers.

## The Model Lesson Plan

Boys need a specific style of instruction that will motivate them to read. There is a consensus among researchers that boys benefit from structured lessons that are based on clear goals and explicit expectations. Other educators have noted that boys need short activities that will keep them moving around the classroom (Lewis and Wray 1997; Millard 1997; Bauer 2001). As Noble and Bradford (2000) have found, "Keep it short, keep it sharp, keep it finite."

What is the ideal lesson model for most boys?

♦ The lesson should be brief: ten to fifteen minutes at the junior level, longer in the later grades.

♦ The format should be consistent from lesson to lesson.

♦ Instructions should be simple and direct so that even the poorest student can understand them.

♦ Lessons should strike a balance between being teacher-directed and student-directed.

♦ Complex lessons should be broken down into smaller sections, where each division is based on one activity.

♦ The lesson should have an element of challenge or competition.

♦ Boys should be given opportunities to work both independently and in groups.

♦ The lesson should end with a period of reflection and review.

| Lesson Model for Grades 7 or 8 Boys | |
| --- | --- |
| Brief introductory activity | 5–10 minutes |
| Discussion with partner, group, or class | 10–15 minutes |
| Reflection and review with partner, group, or class | 10–15 minutes |

Figure 3.2

## Learning Styles

In developing lesson plans, teachers should be aware of the different styles that children have in learning (Figure 3.4 on page 50). Boys and girls share these styles even if they do not always apply them in the same way. (See Figure 3.5 on page 51.)

## Sample Lesson

**Book:** *The Iron Man*

**Author:** Ted Hughes

**Time:** four book-club sessions (one a day), 25–40 minutes each

**Expectations:**

◆ Make predictions while reading a story or novel, using various clues.

◆ Make judgments and draw conclusions about ideas in written materials on the basis of evidence.

**Goals for Reading This Book:**

◆ To actively engage the boys in reading a novel.

◆ To motivate the boys to read, discuss, and think about a novel.

◆ To demonstrate that reading and discussing can be fun!

**Week 1**

◆ Read aloud Chapter 1 of *The Iron Man*, without showing them the book, to "hook" the boys.

◆ Discuss the visualizations they have created in their heads about what the Iron Man looks like as his hand and eye hop around to put the rest of his body together.

**Guided Discussion Time:**

◆ Predict, based on clues from the book, what will happen in the next chapter.

*Inference questions to think about:*

◆ Where is the Iron Man going when he goes out into the sea?

◆ Where did he come from in the first place?

◆ Is it possible for a machine to rebuild itself?

**Assign:**

◆ Chapters 2 and 3 to read on their own before Week 2's session.

◆ Introduce the *Notes to Remember* page, photocopied on cardstock. This is a blank page for students to record their thoughts and observations as they read.

**Teacher Reflection after Book-Club Session:**

Some of the boys had seen *The Iron Giant* movie and were thinking that the book would be exactly like the movie. I advised those students not to make that assumption and to read the book carefully, looking for the differences.

(Gilroy 2005)

Figure 3.3

## Styles of Learning*

| | |
|---|---|
| **Visual Learners** | *Students learn through seeing.* They learn best from visual displays, body language, facial expressions, written information, charts and diagrams, illustrations that reinforce text, and videos. They make up the majority of boy and girl learners, about 65 percent. |
| **Auditory Learners** | *Students learn from the spoken word.* They learn best from listening to what is said in the classroom: the teachers' discourses, class and peer discussions. Because girls are more verbal, they are likely more comfortable with this style of learning. About 35 percent of students are auditory learners. |
| **Kinesthetic Learners** | *Students learn from actively exploring the physical world around them.* Their need for activity and exploration may lead students to become distracted and unable to sit still for long periods of time. They make up about 5 percent of learners, many of whom are boys. |

*Adapted from *Mind Tools* 1999. Note: Some students use more than one style of learning.

Figure 3.4

## Boys' Learning Styles

**Preferred**

- Doing brief, limited tasks
- Learning actively
- Participating in groups
- Doing challenges and competitions
- Doing quizzes
- Discussing and other oral work
- Using technology

**Not Preferred**

- Copying from the board
- Listening to the teacher
- Doing worksheets
- Writing on their own
- Reading on their own

Figure 3.5

Closely linked to these learning styles is the way in which students prefer to work: alone (intrapersonal) or co-operatively (interpersonal). Intrapersonal learners enjoy working independently. They are self-reflective, prefer privacy and quiet when learning, think independently, and are aware of their own feelings. Interpersonal learners learn best in a co-operative environment. They are good organizers, sensible to the feelings and moods of others, and are social rather than solitary. The majority of boys are interpersonal learners. Teachers need to develop alternative ways for students to respond to the curriculum to satisfy this range of learning styles as well as the differences between boy and girl learners.

> "For [students] who are reluctant readers and tactile learners, we must provide a physical component with instruction . . . using . . . anything that gets the physical body involved" (Jobe and Dayton-Sakari 2002, 58).

## Creating the Right Classroom Environment

### The Active Classroom

If there is one word that describes boys in school, it is *active*. Boys need to move around the classroom. As research has shown, they are not good at sitting still and working quietly. That is not to say that pandemonium should be the norm. Boys should have a purpose in moving. Their physical activity should be related to their learning:

♦ sharing information with other students or groups

♦ interviewing other students

♦ making some object, display, or device

♦ doing presentations to a group or class

Boys need to realize that physical activity in the classroom does not have to be equated with misbehaving. The class clown who wants to sit on his desk can become the discussion moderator. The boy who needs to sharpen his pencil every five minutes can become the student who passes out and collects assignments (Gurian 2001, 47).

## The Literate Classroom

A learning environment for boys should reflect what they are doing. If boys are expected to read, they need to see reading material all around them. Classrooms should display fiction and non-fiction books, magazines, newspapers, posters, audio and music CDs, poems and song lyrics, vertical files of student stories and reports, captioned cartoons, indexes of sports cards—anything that interests boy readers. One part of the classroom might be set aside as a library corner (Morrow and O'Connor 1995) where students are encouraged to go during their free class time. There, students can find comfortable chairs, pillows on the floor to sit on, attractive book and magazine displays, writing materials, and recorded reading-lab stories.

## The Co-operative Classroom

Competition may be natural for most boys, but for many students such as Arnold, whom we met in the previous chapter, too much of it can make them anxious and unwilling to participate in class activities. For the teacher, it is a balancing act between encouraging a boy's competitiveness and his social need to be part of a group. Boys should have numerous opportunities to work with partners and in groups. They should be given activities that stress co-operation in learning situations where they share information (for example, where each member of the group contributes one portion of a multitask assignment). Still, competition in the form of games and contests will motivate many boys in doing reading and writing assignments. I have had great success with games such as Family Feud, as well as spelling bees and boys-versus-girls activities.

"Brain researchers have suspected for years now that where a male is in the pecking order may have a great effect on how he learns because of the level of stress hormones [he gets]. . . . Males on the high end . . . [who] secrete less hormone [are better learners]. Males at the bottom end [who] secrete more [hormone are poorer learners]" (Gurian 2001, 48).

When assigning students to groups, it is important to keep in mind the way girls and boys view friendship and group affiliations. Girls do not need an excuse to share ideas and emotions with other girls. Boys need a purpose or an activity. Girls use language to co-operate. Boys do not mind being a member of a hierarchical group, especially one that has a common task or purpose. Yet boys "can spend hours playing a video game without exchanging a complete sentence" (Sax 2005, 83).

Teachers should also be aware of boy behaviour that might make it difficult for them to co-operate. For example:

♦ Boys do not like to ask for help. If a group of boys gets stuck on a task, the boys can easily turn the task into fooling around.

♦ While hierarchical groups are comfortable for boys, too strict a ranking can sometimes lead to bullying.

- Many boys see interaction with their teachers as a sign of male weakness or nerdiness (Gurian 2001, 84).

## The Culture of Reading

Boys need to feel part of a school culture of reading. Creating such a culture means that

- reading permeates the school day from "book talks" on the morning announcements to authors' festivals, book fairs, student publications, sustained silent reading times, and library programs.
- "reading" is the topic of conversation among professionals in the school.
- educators in the school share strategies with one another and ask for assistance in teaching important reading skills.
- staff development focuses on teaching reading instruction across the content areas.
- data on student reading performance, information about reading programs, and useful reading strategies are shared at staff or team meetings.
- parents are informed about how to encourage reading at home.
- local libraries are asked to promote student membership in addition to providing books for students to use in school.

## Supporting Reading Instruction

The instructional methods and strategies that teachers use to teach reading are often going to be different for boys and girls. So, too, are the practices that support this instruction. The following examples outline some of these support practices that might be helpful in teaching boys to read.

## Groups and Partners

Boys like to work in groups because they are comfortable with a peer-group social unit. They also like group work because it reduces individual responsibility for completing a task. However, boys who are not good verbal communicators can feel intimidated by girls who are able to express themselves easily. For these boys, it might be better to include them in all-boys groups where they will be more likely to share ideas (Sax 2002).

That is not to say that separating boys and girls should be the norm for literacy instruction. Many students set their standards of work and behaviour by imitating their peers. Boys might re-evaluate their notions of how well they are doing in class if they have the example of a girl to live up to.

## Reading Aloud

Boys gain confidence in their reading ability when they read aloud in class. They should be encouraged every day to read their own writing, dialogue in drama scripts, and portions of assigned reading and textbooks. Teachers should be aware that frequent interruptions or corrections can undermine boys' confidence. In fact, researchers have found that teachers tend to correct boys' reading more than that of girls (McCarthy et al. 2001; Smith and Wilhelm 2002).

> "Choral reading . . . enables struggling readers to hear fluent reading, and allows them to participate without feeling self-conscious about making mistakes" (Strickland, Ganske, and Monroe 2002, 124).

When teachers read aloud, they can introduce different genres and material that would be too difficult for the boys to read. Teacher read-alouds also are effective because they "model both the 'how' and 'why' of reading" (Ontario Ministry of Education 2003(b), 4.3). They also allow teachers to use such strategies as think-alouds and other verbalizing processes to help boys recognize language cues (ibid.).

## Homework

Homework is important—possibly more so for boys. Girls can process a great deal of learning in the classroom. Boys need more reinforcement. Homework is a way for boys to retain what they have learned in school as well as to improve their critical thinking skills. Because they tend to be task-oriented, they like doing research projects, investigations, interviews, observations, and solving problems. If you ask boys what they think of homework, they will likely say that it is boring and a waste of time. Boys need to see a direct connection between their class work and what they are asked to do at home. In other words, teachers should try to incorporate boys' natural interests into their homework assignments. If boys are given a clear outline of what is expected of them and the purpose of the assignment, they will usually respond with determination and enthusiasm. One practice that I have found successful in encouraging boys to complete their home assignments is to establish a phone or web-based homework hotline. There, students and/or their parents can get immediate help and guidance.

---

### Boys' Homework Assignments*

Boys are more likely to do their homework if the assignment

◆ lets the boys practise skills learned in class.
◆ allows boys to practise skills or learn material that is outside the curriculum expectations, but is related.
◆ encourages boys to brainstorm and think critically.
◆ uses resources found at home.

*Adapted from Pollack and Cushman 2001, 236–237

---

Figure 3.6

## Changing Male Stereotypical Behaviour

Regardless of whether it is biologically or socially determined, many boys ascribe to an image of maleness that is more

> "Every society confronts the problem of civilizing its young males. The traditional approach is through character education: Develop the young man's sense of honor. Help him become a considerate, conscientious human being. . . . This approach respects boys' masculine nature; it is time tested, and it works" (Sommers, May 2000).

"machismo" than intellectual (the "boy code"). As Gambell and Hunter point out (2000, 697), "Boys mime prescribed lines of a time-worn script on the male role, [and] they learn to distance themselves from any activity considered feminine." And that behaviour goes beyond "boys don't cry." Boys also don't read. They don't ask for help in class or at home. In many classes, the boys fool around.

Teachers need to counter these ideas of maleness. I have had success with male mentoring programs (see Boys to Men, pages 74–85), class and school reading programs that utilize men reading aloud (page 72), father and son book clubs, and special programs that target at-risk African-Canadian boys (see Project Pride, pages 70–72). In all these examples, having men read and discuss literature to groups of "machismo" boys has had a great influence on how they perceive reading and education. A young, tough male is not about to call a two-metre-tall Toronto Raptor a "nerd" because he is reading a poem to the class. As Pollack and others have concluded, "Boys benefit enormously from having [male] mentors who are sympathetic to them as learners and who can serve as models for what it's possible to achieve" (Pollack 1998, 268).

## Reading and Writing Connections

Writing is a complement to reading. Boys need to understand that someone has put words on the page for them to read. Indeed, writers are always reading over what they have written. That is the process of revising and editing. It is not surprising that ministry documents on reading suggest that "classroom instruction should develop and enhance a reciprocal relationship between reading and writing" (Ontario Ministry of Education 2003(b), 10.3). As Tyrone, who is in grade 3 tells it, "I love to write. I do lots of reading, and that's how I learned to write." Performances on provincial tests seem to suggest this connection. Good readers are usually good writers, the opposite being true as well (Ontario Ministry of Education 2004(b), 13; EQAO 2004, 18).

Writing offers boys opportunities to express their ideas without having to speak extemporaneously. It also offers teachers glimpses into how and what boys think and feel. For these reasons, boys need to develop a sense of trust with the people in their writing community. This is especially true for those who have problems with literacy.

Boys also need to be exposed to reading material that will serve as models for good writing. They should see adults engaged in the act of writing and view their teachers as writing collaborators.

Reading a good book or story can inspire a student to be a better writer. So will allowing students choice in what they read and write. Get boys to write about something that interests them. Have them read it aloud. Then point out to them, "Now you are reading!"

The buddy program for reading can be very successful with boys. Pair an older boy who is struggling with reading with a young reluctant or novice reader. Both boys will benefit from this pairing: the older boy will feel important and a more able reader compared to the younger child; the younger boy will have a mentor to emulate. They can read together, work on reading strategies, and write and prepare a booklet based on the younger child's interests.

# 4

# Outreach Programs for At-Risk Boys

> *"Deciding to go into teaching must be a decision from the heart. It must come from a moral imperative to ensure the success of all children and from a commitment to social justice" (Spence 2002, 142).*

## Deficit-Model Students

Against the advice of many of my friends, I began my teaching career at a high-needs middle school in Toronto. I wanted to reach students who had somehow slipped through the cracks of the educational system. However, nothing I had encountered at teachers' college could have prepared me for what I first faced in the classroom, and for a brief moment, I thought my friends had been right. Students routinely came to school without pen or paper, and they *never* took home their school books. There were students who could not write their names, read simple paragraphs, or answer basic math problems. At best, they were apathetic toward learning; at worst, disruptive.

> "Struggling readers and writers often find themselves caught in a cycle of failure. They have difficulty learning to read and write, so they avoid literacy activities. Avoidance means they don't get the practice they need to strengthen their skills" (Strickland, Ganske, and Monroe 2002, 13).

A few of the teachers had given up on these students. They viewed them by what I began to call the "deficit model": the students were labelled by their deficiencies. And the students did lack a great deal. Many of them were new immigrants. Like their parents, they had little or no English language skills. Some students came from single-parent homes where there wasn't always food on the table or a safe bed to sleep in. The students and their families were so caught up in the business of surviving, they hadn't the energy for learning. Consequently, the young people fitted into the deficit model by which these teachers defined them: they did poorly in all aspects of school life. I felt I knew otherwise.

Fortunately for me, I had a supportive principal, and there were many committed and exceptional teachers at the school. We all spent that year working long hours to improve our students' school performances and attitudes towards learning. We conducted special classes on the weekends, school nights, and even during school holidays. We bought meals for them, often took the place of disinterested parents when they needed adult support, and gave up our evenings and weekends to drive them to special events. We knew these students were able to learn and were determined to prove it.

And we did!

One of my first classes was a grade 6 all-boys group. Most of the students were black. Many of them had no male role model in their lives. They were so used to getting D's and F's that they looked upon school only as a place to meet their friends. But during that year, we changed all that. They came into my class with the lowest math test scores in the school. When the year ended, they had one of the highest. When I held classes on Saturdays, every student attended. I had high expectations for them and so did they of themselves. I was impressed with their commitment to learn, and they were impressed with my commitment to teach them.

What I learned in those first few years of teaching was that a teacher had to *begin* with the student. I was constantly asking myself, "Who are my learners and what are their needs?" I realized that there was no sense in showing them long division if they could not add or subtract and no point in explaining how to develop a paragraph if they could barely read a sentence.

Schools have never set out to be surrogate parents or counselling centres. They are supposed to be places for learning. But for these at-risk students, learning was never going to take place unless they saw the point of it—unless they viewed their teachers as mentors, not antagonists. That meant that we, as teachers, had to get personally involved. As our students told us, we had to "walk the walk, talk the talk."

I had one student who became withdrawn whenever we were doing math. The boy rarely took risks if he thought he might fail or be wrong, and he knew very little mathematics. I wondered how I could reach him. Then I discovered that he had a huge baseball card collection. I thought that if I could use his card collection as a basis for doing math, he might eventually change his attitude toward the subject.

I began by suggesting to him that he organize his cards by player position. Then I asked him questions about his organization—for example: How many shortstops do you have? how many pitchers? and so on. Next, we discussed what the numbers on the back of the cards represented. Although he had collected the cards for years, he had no idea. He was fascinated when I told him that they were the players' career statistics. I got him working on simple problems that involved these statistics: how many total strikeouts a player had for a given set of years, how many two-base hits, etc. I had him compare one player's statistics to another's. He even began asking me questions about various player's statistics, and we worked out the answers together. And at no time did I mention the word "math."

There were other boys in that class who also collected and traded baseball cards. I organized an after-school club where we all asked each other questions about their cards. I still didn't talk about the "m" word because that might have spoiled the fun, but they were discovering number sense. All the while, I insisted that the boys adhere to strict discipline guidelines. We were not getting together to fool around, even if the activities we did were fun. They had no trouble with my rules. They knew I cared about them. They respected me and wanted to live up to my expectations for them—which were high.

> "Believe that all students can be joyful, independent readers and writers . . . and that you can help them reach that goal" (Taylor and Doyle Collins 2003, 3).

But the challenges were great among the students I taught. I remember asking one student what he was going to do when he grew up and eventually left the neighbourhood. He was surprised by my question. "This is my home," he said. "I have always lived here. I guess I always will." The possibility of an alternative lifestyle had never occurred to him. Over time, I felt an immense sadness from these kinds of revelations, and I became determined to expand this limited view for as many students as possible.

## Reaching Out

As I discovered in my first few years of teaching, to be effective with at-risk students required commitments outside the classroom and curriculum. This reaching out—this listening to what students had to say and then *doing* something about it—meant that I had to approach teaching them differently from the traditional methodology I had learned at teachers' college. My colleagues and I came to realize that our commitments to these students needed to be transformed into formal outreach programs that were more organized than our initial efforts. Like my baseball-card club, these programs needed to reach and teach children where classroom instruction had been unsuccessful. And because a majority of these students were boys, many of the programs became, in effect, boys' clubs.

When I became principal of Lawrence Heights Middle School in Toronto, I had more opportunities to utilize school- and Toronto Board-wide outreach programs. Lawrence Heights was an inner-city school where many of the boys and girls had the characteristics of at-risk students (see Figure 4.1). They came from over thirty countries and spoke as many as twenty-five different languages. In a school year, there were nearly 3000 lates and hundreds of

"Schools exist for children, not for the benefit of the adults who work in them. Thus the focus of restructuring and reform efforts must be to enhance the benefits for children" (Allington and Walmsley 1995, 258).

## Identifying At-Risk Learners

Most at-risk students usually have one or more of the following characteristics:

◆ They are often boys.

◆ They have poor academic skills.

◆ They have negative images of themselves.

◆ They have been diagnosed with learning and/or behaviour difficulties.

◆ They come from low-income families.

◆ They come from families where standard English is a second language or dialect.

◆ They come from single-parent families.

◆ They come from families where the parents have poor academic skills and/or less than a high school education.

Figure 4.1

> "Being genuinely literate entails more than simply scoring well on a standardized test, and it definitely involves more than learning a narrow range of reading and editing skills. It entails actively engaging in literate behavior" (Walp and Walmsley 1995, 180).

students sent home for one reason or another. There were fights in the schoolyard and drug dealers in the neighbourhood. But in two years, student lates were reduced to less than 500 and academic achievement had improved. Where once more than half the teachers left to go to other schools, we had a waiting list of teachers wanting to join the staff. This turnaround came about because of the fierce dedication and high expectations of our teachers and staff and because of the many in-school and extracurricular programs for the students.

We developed a strategic plan that served as a basis for our school philosophy and also guided our thinking for our programs. The basis for this plan had a number of tenets:

- Each child can learn.
- Each child is important and unique.
- Everyone has a right to feel safe at school.
- People will support, value, and respect what they help to create themselves.
- Establishing short- and long-term goals for students is essential for student success.
- Diversity strengthens the individual, the school, and the community.
- There exists a direct relationship between expectations and achievement.
- Education is a shared responsibility of students, educators, parents, and people in the community.

We did not just believe in these statements, we put our beliefs into practice.

## Developing Literacy Outreach Programs

### Developmental Stages

We learned a great deal at Lawrence Heights about how to create and use outreach programs. Later, when I thought about all we had accomplished, I realized that we had actually gone through three stages of development in implementing our programs. Our initial efforts had mostly been individual ones, like my card club. But more team planning had become necessary as the programs became more complex and varied. We also began to utilize people from outside our classrooms and the school, which required further planning and coordination. And, of course, at every step of the way, we sought the advice and support of central office staff and administrators.

As the stages suggest (see Figure 4.2 on next page), we started modestly and built upon these beginnings until we were involved in a complex system of programs with a variety of professional and volunteer personnel.

### Leadership in Literacy Programs

To be effective, literacy programs need to be school- and board-wide. Literacy instruction should not be something that occurs only during language arts periods. It needs to be part of the students' school life. It should be ongoing, regular, and—at least for at-risk boys—associated with predictable activities.

As I found at Lawrence Heights, any school-wide literacy program requires careful planning, thoughtful monitoring, and a great deal of collaboration with staff, students, board administrators, and the community. Leadership is important in establishing these programs, although it does not necessarily have to come from the school principal or consultants. Regardless of who the organizers are, educators have identified a number of conditions

| Implementing Outreach Programs for At-Risk Students* | | | |
|---|---|---|---|
| | **Stage 1** | **Stage 2** | **Stage 3** |
| Learning Strategies | Use one or two learning strategies; for example, a small group of students works with a parent volunteer. | Determine that a number of strategies are needed for individual and/or small groups of students. | Plan and implement a wide variety of learning strategies to meet student needs. |
| Use of Personnel | Enlist a few specialized people. | Access assistance within and outside the classroom. | Actively engage school and community personnel to deliver a wide variety of learning strategies and programs. |

*Adapted from *Literacy Guidelines Implementation Stages* (Hamilton-Wentworth DSB 2003, 13–14)

Figure 4.2

that need to be met to ensure a program's success (The Knowledge Loom 2002):

**Clear goals need to be established**—The program goals must specifically deal with the strategies needed to improve student literacy. Without these goals being clearly stated, it is easy for programs to become sidetracked by student issues other than literacy.

**The program's priorities and resources need to be communicated**—Messages to teachers and students about the importance of literacy need to come from school and board administrators, literacy program organizers, curriculum specialists, and mentors, as well as the students' adult family members. School administrators should also communicate their support by providing classroom space and materials for programs and, if necessary, adjusting timetables to accommodate the program.

**Literacy should be part of every school-wide program**— Teachers need to be encouraged to include literacy instruction in content areas and activities other than language arts. For example, older student tutors might participate in shared-reading activities for subjects like science or social studies. Schools can have book fairs and book clubs that emphasize how-to information materials (books, magazines, etc.) rather than literary genres. School-wide periods of silent and shared reading can be scheduled for all students. Events such as career days could be centred around reading material (brochures, instructional manuals related to careers, etc.).

**Ongoing professional development on literacy should be provided**—Time should be set aside at staff meetings and during professional development days for information about literacy instruction. Teachers need opportunities to share success stories, talk about teaching strategies, discuss the latest research, and review literacy programs and student achievement. Curriculum needs to be developed or adapted to meet the needs of the programs.

**Literacy programs need to be formally reviewed and evaluated**—School and board programs should be monitored in order to

♦ examine learning outcomes and student results.

♦ review the effectiveness of program components.

♦ obtain participant feedback.

Unlike professional development discussions, the review process should occur on a regular basis (weekly, monthly, etc.). Reports should also be issued and shared with other educators.

> "Some boys need to talk through their ideas before they are sure they understand what they have read and before they can commit their ideas to paper effectively. Failing to provide for this social component, for the opportunity to verbalize ideas before reading or writing about them, can create a problem for some boys" (Ontario Ministry of Education 2004(b), 26).

What follows are brief descriptions of some of the outreach programs with which I have been involved, as well as a detailed look at the Boys to Men mentoring program. Most of these programs focus on pre-adolescent and adolescent boys, many of whom are at-risk students. While some programs did not specifically centre on literacy, their activities were often language-based and so were effective in getting boys to read and write. After all, students who struggle with literacy need constant practice. They need to feel confident enough to have "the stamina to continue reading difficult texts" (Beers 2003, 18).

## Outreach Programs

### School Book Clubs

Book clubs are a way of exposing boys to a wider variety of reading material than they might otherwise be accustomed to reading. Activities in the clubs can take many forms but are often similar to the book talks teachers give in class:

♦ The cover of the book is shown and discussed.

♦ The genre the book represents is explained.

♦ Information about the book's author is provided.

♦ A summary of the book is given that will entice students to read it.

(Strickland, Ganske, and Monroe 2002, 79)

While boys' book clubs can use the above model as a basis for their talks, it is the boys who do the talking, not the teacher. Boys are encouraged to bring to the club's discussions their interests and knowledge of their home and community. Thus, the reading material introduced probably will not be limited to fiction, or even to books. The boys might want to share an article on fixing something (e.g., on reconditioning a used bike), or they might have found an article on the Internet that explains something about a hobby (e.g., how to grind lenses to make a telescope). What is often emphasized in boys' book clubs is that reading need not only be a solitary activity. It can be an opportunity to share and discuss. Boys will discover that sharing what they read can help them better understand what they read.

It is important, when dealing with at-risk boys, for organizers to establish the parameters of the book club. For example, I would explain to them what is appropriate to discuss about their reading material and how they should conduct themselves during the discussion. I would also talk about strategies for keeping the talks going, how to respond to questions, how to clarify their ideas and opinions, and how to ask good questions.

As with all outreach programs, there are certain characteristics that make book clubs successful. Some are listed below.

♦ *High Expectations*—Participants (and their teachers) need to believe that they will be able to appreciate and understand what they read. Boys should be encouraged to bring reading material from their homes. As well, teachers can help students by ensuring that they have a variety of in-class reading material that suits the boys' ages and reading abilities.

♦ *Non-Judgmental Attitudes*—Club members should be part of a literacy environment where they can freely express their reading preferences. Boys especially need to be able to read material they enjoy and not fear that they will be judged by their choices.

- *Free Time*—Time needs to be set aside during the school day for book-club activities. As well, space has to be made available for clubs to meet (a corner of the library, an unused room, etc.).

- *Direct Instruction*—Book clubs represent another opportunity outside of formal class time to introduce reading and writing strategies.

- *Modelling and Scaffolding*—As part of direct instruction, teachers and students can discuss and give examples for literary models. For example, students might explain how they went about doing a book report or why they have chosen a particular piece of writing they thought was excellent or important to them.

Many boy book clubs also follow a model (based on that of Raphael and her colleagues) that consists of four elements:

- small-group discussions
- whole-class discussions
- individual reading sessions
- individual writing sessions

(McMahon et al. 1997; Raphael 1999; Raphael, Ruane, and George 2001)

Given the chance, boys will be eager to express their reading preferences as well as be open to material with which they are unfamiliar.

## Project Pride

### Background

When I was principal of Lawrence Heights, we began an outreach program for African-Canadian students called Project Pride. We were concerned with the academic underachievement and social problems of many of the black male students. A variety of factors had been cited for their underachievement, including socio-economic conditions, family structure, and peer pressure. Whatever the causes, research has shown that schools can make a difference in the lives of the urban poor (Edmonds 1979). One of the features of a successful school for black students is that the teaching staff strive to improve the self-image of its students. Self-esteem is important for all students, but for underachieving African-Canadians, it is particularly important. As American social psychologist Claude Steel has written, "The underachievement of [black students] stems not from limitations in their innate ability to achieve and succeed in school, but from systemic discrimination" (Steel 1992, 4). It is this discrimination that erodes self-esteem and "insulates them from the failure of academic life" (ibid.).

"All children are profoundly affected by role models. Unfortunately, the male role models boys encounter in popular culture—in movies, television, and video games—often do not appear to engage in or value reading and writing" (Ontario Ministry of Education 2004(b), 30).

Project Pride tried to counter these realities for young blacks. The program challenged them to assume some of the responsibility for their circumstances, regardless of the discrimination they might face. It also challenged them to succeed academically as well as to provide leadership for their families, school, and community. Similar to Boys to Men (see pages 74–85), it emphasized that "excuses are for losers."

## The Program

To get the program started, I had staff members identify twenty African-Canadian boys who were socially and academically at risk. Once a working group of staff members and students was established, parents and caregivers were informed about the program. Boys and the staff members then got together to discuss the direction and mission of the program. Next, each boy was assigned a staff member to serve as a mentor. The mentors undertook the following tasks:

- Communicated daily with the boy.
- Communicated weekly with the home (a minimum of two phone calls home to a parent or the boy).
- Monitored homework and class-assignment completion; helped with preparing for tests and doing assignments.
- Acted as a liaison between the boy and other staff members.
- Developed an educational and personal plan for the boy.
- Got together with other mentors for discussions as the need arose.

Project Pride could very well serve as a model for any outreach program that targets at-risk students.

## Read to Succeed

"The more you read, the more you know. The more you know, the further you go. So read . . . read . . . read!" This was the theme for one of the Read to Succeed conferences organized through the Toronto District School Board. The conference was for the hundreds of grades 3 and 6 boys and their teachers who participated in book clubs. Everyone met at a high-tech game arcade for a day of fun and literacy. There, the boys listened to "boy" writers, such as Eric Walters and Christopher Paul Curtis, met male sports celebrities who promoted reading, played video games, and ate pizza. As explained in the letter sent home to the boys' parents:

> We are committed to helping the young men in our respective Families of Schools succeed in school. We recognize that one of the areas in which some boys are falling behind is in the area of literacy, particularly reading. This conference has been designed to encourage our grades three and six boys to recognize the joy and power of reading. We are confident that once boys realize the importance that reading brings to their future, they will find ways to incorporate it into their lives.

The message to parents was that their boys did not have to abandon one activity for the sake of another. They could play sports and video games, hang out with friends, *and* still find time to read.

The idea for these conferences stems from the notion of a culturally relevant approach to literacy teaching (Ladson-Billings 1995). This approach involves talking to students about the personal value of choosing academic achievement. (To this end, we surveyed over 300 boys.) Learning activities are based on the students' cultural norms and experiences. In effect, learning becomes a social activity. Thus, holding a reading conference at a video arcade—not a typical place of learning— illustrated this approach. By talking about literacy in the context of the boys' social milieu, a statement about reading was made: reading is just as normal as playing video games. Judging by the enthusiasm the boys expressed for reading, the conference was a success.

> "We don't know what the world will look like next year, much less in a decade from now. I think that part of our task in raising sons is to give them the tools for developing their values so that, as times change, they will have the tools for making informed, responsible choices throughout their life" (Kivel 1999, 34).

## Boys to Men

### Program Background

Boys to Men is a mentoring program that attempts to guide, support, and nurture at-risk boys. The program was started at Oakdale Park Middle School in Toronto in the early 1990s. Now there are over thirty chapters in Toronto, plus six school chapters in the Hamilton-Wentworth School District. While it has often been a mission of mine to work to improve the self-image of African Canadian youth, programs such as Boys to Men are not based on race or ethnic background. Indeed, when the Hamilton chapters were first established in 2004, 75 percent of the boys identified as at-risk students were *not* Black. Social and economic factors are what put students at risk, not ethnicity or skin colour.

It is the belief of the Boys to Men program that some at-risk boys need to emulate and be tutored by male role models. Otherwise, they are likely to act the way 11-year-old Marlon describes his behaviour at school:

| | |
|---|---|
| *Researcher:* | *How are you doing in school?* |
| Marlon: | Okay, I guess. . . . Sometimes I get in trouble. |
| *Researcher:* | *What do you do to get into trouble?* |
| Marlon: | I don't know . . . just stuff . . . stuff that makes the class laugh. You know . . . fun stuff. |
| *Researchers:* | *Like telling jokes?* |
| Marlon: | Yeah . . . but other stuff, too. Like, I don't know . . . throwing stuff. |
| *Researcher:* | *Why do you think you do that?* |
| Marlon: | Just for fun, I guess. |
| *Researcher:* | *Marlon, do you know why the teacher has to constantly stop the class to stop you from fooling around?* |
| Marlon: | No. (*He looks sad when he answers.*) |
| *Researcher:* | *You want to know what I think? I think you want to be noticed more in the class.* |
| Marlon: | I don't know. Maybe. (*He smiles.*) |

I agree with Michael Gurian when he says that "without male role models, boy culture feels lost. [If it] is not mentored by spiritually vital elder males, [it] is more a gang than a culture" (Gurian 1996, 44). Mentoring programs such as Boys to Men help boys like Marlon find their way out of misbehaving and failure at school.

Another aspect of Boys to Men clubs is that they offer boys alternative places in which to hang out. At-risk boys often live in an unsafe world. They spend their out-of-school time unsupervised on the streets, in the malls, and with older, sometimes criminal youths. They need safe environments where they won't feel intimidated by other "boy code" males.

A word of caution to those educators who are unfamiliar with boy culture and boys' clubs. This is a hierarchical world that includes far more discipline and ritual than is found in today's classroom. For example, at the Hamilton-Wentworth District School Board Boys to Men meetings, each meeting begins with a different boy reciting the club creed (Figure 4.3). He then listens as the other boys and men repeat it back.

"A destiny of aggression isn't born, it's made, most notably in societies like ours in which aggressive impulses are allowed free rein. We can raise boys to be nonviolent if we so choose" (Kindlon 2000, 14).

As for the objectives of the program, they are as much concerned with discipline and the consequences of ignoring this discipline as they are with the social, moral, and academic improvement of the boys. Without clear rules,

---

### Boys to Men Creed

As boys transitioning to men, we must *respect* ourselves and others. We must take *pride* in rebuilding our community. We must act with *dignity* and character.

---

Figure 4.3

many at-risk boys will push the limits of acceptable behaviour until they start "throwing stuff."

Thus the objectives of the program—and these are openly discussed when the boys and men get together—are succinct:

- Change unacceptable behaviour.

- Become academically successful.

- Form a bond with a mentor.

- Find an alternative lifestyle.

- Learn to be responsible for your actions.

## Boys to Men: Guiding Principles

**Mentors serve as role models**—Mentors are the foundation of Boys to Men. Similar in concept to Big Brothers, mentors offer boys positive images of male adulthood. Teachers, coaches, staff advisers, school administrators, and educational assistants have been successful mentors.

The mentoring groups are typically small, no more than six to ten students for each adult. Once a mentor has been selected, teachers and parents of the boys in that group are informed that the boys will be involved in the program.

---

### Mentoring: Criteria for Success

- *Establish the length of the relationship.* Mentors and boys should commit themselves for a period of between six months and one year.

- *Stay in contact.* Many programs set a minimum of one contact per week between boys and mentors. Other programs have minimum levels of attendance at scheduled program activities.

- *Commit to a level of personal involvement.* The mentors and boys determine the depth to which their relationship will develop.

---

Figure 4.4

**Boys are initiated into manhood**—The initiation rites of the program direct and dignify the transition from boyhood to manhood. These rites include learning new information, adhering to rules of conduct, setting personal goals, and providing community service. Like it or not, teachers need to realize that much of boy culture today is based on a code of behaviour that initiates boys into what Paul Kivel calls the " 'Act Like a Man' box" (1999, 11–14). Similar in concept to the "boy code," boys "in the box" are expected to emulate the manly characteristics of toughness, aggressiveness, and stoicism. Certainly, these images are portrayed in the media and by many male sports figures. Boys are assessed as being either "in the box" (as a man) or "outside the box" (as a "wimp, sissy, mama's boy, girl, fag, nerd, punk, mark, [or] bitch" (ibid., 11). The objective of Boys to Men is to replace these attitudes with those that will allow the boys to grow into "responsible, co-operative, caring, and competent" men (ibid., 15).

**Boys gain self-esteem**—The assumption the program makes is that at-risk boys' self-esteem has been eroded by the "boy code"/ Man in the Box definition of masculinity. Low self-esteem has been linked to poor school performance and the school dropout rate. As one Toronto District School Board trustee admitted to me, schools "have become somewhat lethargic about adolescent self-esteem, yet it goes to the core of why so many adolescents get into trouble and drop out of school." Indeed, the school dropout rate in Ontario in 2004 had reached 30 percent (Brown 2005).

To counter these feelings of low self-esteem, boys are helped with their schoolwork, taught non-violent conflict resolution strategies, and given the opportunity to discuss responsible sexual behaviour.

**The consequences of behaviour are explained**—In the program, boys are expected to understand the consequences of not doing well in school or quitting altogether. Students need to realize that without enough education, they may have to settle for a lifetime of labouring jobs. Thus, the boys and their mentors work together to develop a system of social values and skills that will facilitate success in school and the workplace.

**The program offers a safe haven**—The program attempts to protect boys at risk by extending the school day. In effect, it tries to keep the boys away from the negative aspects of their lives, such as hanging around in gangs, by providing a place to go after school. Boys are naturally active and physical. They need to express their physicality in an atmosphere where adults "have a reasonable tolerance level for boys' energy" (Kindlon and Thompson 2000, 246).

The overall purpose of the clubs is to give these at-risk boys a lifestyle alternative. Through its activities, it attempts to not only keep the boys off the streets, but also to encourage them to see that becoming successful in school is a goal worth achieving.

## Preplanning the Program

Boys to Men programs need careful planning and monitoring to be successful. Details such as the size of the club (how many mentors and boys), its duration, its typical activities, and target population need to be worked out in advance.

---

### Boys to Men Program Planning

◆ Determine program design.
◆ Establish clear rules and expectations.
◆ Develop program goals.
◆ Create an action plan.

---

Figure 4.5

The following steps in planning have proved successful for most Boys to Men programs:

**Determine program design**—Meet with stakeholders and, together, decide on your program design. For example, discuss the following questions:

- What do you hope to accomplish?
- Whom do you want to reach?
- How do you intend to structure the program?
- Where will you operate the program?
- How will you fund the operating costs?

**Establish clear rules and expectations**—Ensure that your program philosophy and rules are easy for boys to understand, implement, and follow. For instance, you need to determine the answers to questions such as:

- Will mentoring take place in group situations or on a one-to-one basis?
- Will all activities take place just on weekdays after school hours, or will there be some weekend activities?

**Develop your program goals**—Be realistic and set goals that can be attained and evaluated. For example:

- Provide a stable, supportive relationship for youth.
- Show young boys a variety of career opportunities and alternative lifestyles.
- Help prevent boys from dropping out of school.
- Encourage boys to improve their academic performance.
- Help alleviate some of the social problems that affect young boys.
- Help develop emotional intelligence.

**Set objectives**—Given the program, consider

♦ deciding what types of activities you want to promote, such as tutoring, character-building exercises, career field trips, opportunities for social interaction, values clarification exercises, reading assignments, practising of communication skills.

♦ holding events that encourage parents to get involved in the program.

♦ providing training and orientation for mentors, young people, parents, and others involved in the program.

♦ evaluating and monitoring your program's progress and success.

**Create an action plan**—Ensure that your program goals and objectives include plans for

♦ creating a timeline and strategies for recruiting mentors.

♦ hosting a kick-off event.

♦ orienting mentors, youth, and parents.

♦ training mentors and their young partners.

♦ developing a calendar for regular and special events; for example, monthly meetings for mentors to discuss successes and frustrations, or opportunities for youth to offer suggestions for new ways of doing things.

♦ developing a process for continually evaluating the program's effectiveness; for example, determining how many mentor/youth relationships are still going strong after one month, two months, a year.

♦ creating a plan for publicizing and promoting the program.

♦ holding an event to recognize the accomplishments of the program.

## Establishing the Program

Participants usually meet weekly and spend the first week of the program getting to know their mentors. On the first day, there is no talk of rules, no prejudgments made. Only three questions are discussed and answered:

- What is a mentor?
- What would your ideal mentor do for you?
- What adult male do you look up to at school?

The answers to these questions allow the boys to create a list of needs to be attended to throughout the term of the program. Typically, boys want their mentors to help them mature, listen to them, be their friend, teach them new things, and, most surprisingly, be "hard" on them.

---

### Tips for Mentoring Programs

**Be Realistic**

Mentoring does not solve the boys' personal problems. However, it is an invaluable tool for helping young people find the best in themselves and to live up to their potential.

**Think Big, but Start Small**

No matter what size the Boys to Men group is, set realistic growth goals. If the program is good to begin with, it will expand naturally. By then, there should be adequate resources and support to handle the growth.

**Use Existing Resources Rather Than Going It Alone**

Boys to Men groups have contact lists of other participating schools. Help is just a telephone call or e-mail away.

**Look for Ways to Accommodate People's Needs**

Know your school and student needs and capabilities. Keep them in mind when establishing the scope of the program.

---

Figure 4.6

The sessions that follow the first meeting begin with a routine similar to the one below, although this may vary from club to club:

♦ The creed is read and recited.

♦ A question is thrown out for discussion. Each participant is required to contribute his own answer or opinion.

♦ Weekly themes are used to make the sessions more interesting, challenging, and educational.

♦ Each meeting ends with a summarization of the session's goals and objectives.

Many chapters—for example at the high school level—begin with a 45-minute session where the mentors help their boys with homework. These meeting are usually followed up with telephone calls home to update parents on their sons' progress. The homework sessions then expand to leadership opportunities such as helping at parents' night or at school assemblies and activities. Some mentors take their boys to movies, dinners, sports events, as well as attending district-wide Boys to Men anchor events. Anchor events allow students the chance to hear community leaders in education, the arts, and sports. Throughout the program, the boys are monitored to measure their progress with respect to school attendance, academic achievement, and school and home behaviour. Information is gathered anecdotally and from questionnaires. The purpose and objectives of the program are serious ones and the mentors do not pretend otherwise. There is a "bottom line" for everything that the boys do, as I often explained to them:

> ♦ "The important thing is to engage in activities with our students that allow us to get to know them and that communicates our care and concern for them as whole people" (Smith and Wilhelm 2002, 21).

## The Bottom Line

◆ Face it, nobody owes you a living.

◆ Whatever you achieve or fail to achieve in your lifetime is directly related to what you do, or fail to do.

◆ People don't choose their parents or childhood, but you can choose your own direction.

◆ Everyone has problems and obstacles to overcome, but those, too, are relative to each individual.

◆ Nothing is carved into stone. You can change anything in your life if you want to badly enough.

◆ Excuses are for losers. Those who take responsibility for their actions are the real winners in life.

◆ Winners meet life's challenges head on, knowing there are no guarantees. They give all they've got.

◆ Never think it's too early to begin. Time plays no favourites. It will pass whether you act or not.

◆ Take control of your life. Dare to dream and take risks. Compete in life.

Figure 4.7

The initial objective of the mentors is to get the boys talking and to be good listeners to what they have to say. Later, activities are introduced that further engage the boys and get them to express their opinions. For example, at one chapter, a movie such as *Rudy* might be shown. It deals with many of the situations and issues that the boys often confront: parental support, sibling rivalry, mentoring, and goal setting. The showing of the movie can be divided into five segments, with each group of boys conducting "Movie Reviews": They answer questions about the movie that require them to pay attention to the movie's themes. In doing so, the boys are practising good classroom behaviour without realizing it: raising their hands to speak, listening quietly when someone is talking, developing opinions, and answering questions.

Children respond positively to caring adults, as the participants in Boys to Men have shown. In the program are the boys who will become better sons, eventually men, and hopefully mentors to other boys. I am proud that many of them have become men whom I now call my friends. Perhaps it is a cliché to keep repeating to them that they can achieve anything they set their minds and hearts on doing, but the mentors believe it. And so do the boys.

This is what I tell them:

---

### Believe You Can Achieve: *The Game Plan*

*Beliefs are very powerful, so you have to be careful about what you choose to believe, especially about yourself.*

◆ **The Dream**

"[Some people] see things [as they are] and say, 'Why?'. . . . I dream things that never were and . . . say, 'Why not?'" (Shaw 1921)

◆ **Defining the Dream**

The difference between a goal and a dream is the written word.

◆ **Visualizing the Dream**

Visualize every possible step and every subsequent outcome. Visualize what you want to happen: the presentation, the meeting, the encounter.

◆ **Focusing on the Dream**

Practise focusing on positive thoughts and learn to ask yourself effective questions that will lead to effective answers.

◆ **Pursuing the Dream**

Being successful doesn't come to you. You have to go out and get it.

◆ **The Success Zone**

Nothing lasts forever, not success, not failure.

---

Figure 4.8

There have been many successes for the program, but I have always liked the example below. It may sound modest, but for this at-risk boy, it was monumental.

> Once the caretaker of Lawrence Heights was shovelling what seemed like mountains of snow before the arrival of students and staff. As he was battling the drifts and blowing snow, a young man offered his help. His name was Dante, and he was a grade 8 student. He had no gloves, no hat, no boots and was wearing a coat that didn't seem suitable for the weather. Despite what he was wearing, he shovelled the driveway and all the sidewalks. When the caretaker offered to pay him for his work, Dante refused, saying only that he was in Boys to Men. They did not accept money for their good deeds.

# 5

# Leadership and Community Involvement in Education

> *"Schools that provide a school-wide focus on literacy and strong leadership in improving boys' literacy achievements can profoundly affect results in the classroom. Literacy-focused schools assess underachieving groups, identify priorities, and create an action plan to address them"* *(Ontario Ministry of Education 2004(b), 52).*

## Leadership and Literacy Programs

It may seem unusual to conclude a book on boys' literacy with a discussion of leadership roles and responsibilities, but it is appropriate. Without strong leadership at every level of the educational system, little is going to change for the unsuccessful student. In fact, without an understanding of what leadership is, outreach programs will have a poor chance of being effective.

There are many curriculum documents that acknowledge the problem of male literacy and offer advice on how to improve it. However, many boys still have problems with literacy and the dropout rate of boys in secondary schools across the country remains high. So why do some schools have greater success in improving male literacy and keeping students in school? Why are there successful outreach programs in some schools and not in others, when educators in both schools have the same commitment to improving the students' learning?

It is easy to talk about improving the educational environment for unsuccessful learners, but it is another matter to effect these changes. Educators have attended workshops based on statements like "Schools that provide a school-wide focus on literacy and *strong leadership* in improving boys' literacy achievements can profoundly affect results in the classroom" (Ontario Ministry of Education 2004(b), 52 [italics added]). They have read the research and discussed the possible solutions. But when it comes to action, who is going to effect the needed changes? What is *strong leadership* and where will it come from? And if there are strong leaders and successful programs, what is the guarantee that they will still be around next year or ten years down the road?

I find it disheartening to hear about a successful learning program that *used to exist*. I have seen what happens to innovative approaches to teaching disadvantaged students when the initiators leave the school. The sense of purpose is lost or changed and the students drift away. Frontline teachers need support in their efforts to overcome substandard boy literacy. The boys need support not only from one particularly effective teacher, but also support that follows them from grade to grade and school to school. The teachers and students, and the programs in which they participate, need strong leadership from their administrators and colleagues.

## Leadership Responsibilities

Leadership in school districts has many layers, from the director's responsibilities to superintendents, from principals' responsibilities to their teachers. In effective school systems, each person in charge takes responsibility for his or her administrative duties and shares these duties with others. This sharing of leadership is based on a model that I have found to be very successful in educational institutions. Administrators become leaders of leaders, not leaders of followers. They serve as facilitators and moderators, assimilating the ideas of their team members in order to develop the team's plans and strategies. Strong leaders set objectives and goals that accurately reflect the people and programs for which they are intended. In doing so, they have a number of responsibilities to fulfill in order to be effective leaders (see Figure 5.1 below).

For example, directors should develop a senior leadership team that is able to reflect and promote the policies and objectives of

## The Responsibilities of a School Leader

◆ *Get the right people.* Leaders cannot do everything themselves. They need good people in key roles of responsibility.

◆ *Get accurate data.* Organizations succeed or flounder on the information they gather and interpret.

◆ *Get an effective delivery system.* Having the right people and good ideas is not much good if you cannot deliver your programs and practices to the students who need them.

◆ *Get logical systems up and running.* The ability to move information and practices from one place to another—when they are needed—is often the difference between success and failure.

◆ *Get a communication system that works.* Leaders need to be able to communicate effectively both within and outside the organization.

◆ *Get evaluative methods in place.* Organizations need to develop systems of evaluation. They need to determine 1) that the first five responsibilities are acted upon; 2) the strengths and weaknesses of practices (see Figure 5.3 on page 91); and 3) the effectiveness of the personnel involved.

◆ *Realize that successful leadership is a process, not a destination.* Leaders need to be prepared to re-evaluate their understanding of what they are doing and the purpose of their programs and activities.

Figure 5.1

> "Principals are instructional leaders and literacy champions for their school. They align the school's culture and vision with the board's vision for literacy achievement. They encourage strong connections between families and the whole school community" Ontario Ministry of Education 2004(a), 94).

the board. Superintendents should spend significant time in schools and classrooms in their districts to gather information. Principals should work with teachers to develop assessment methods that reflect the students' abilities. These responsibilities may appear to have little connection with the classroom environment, but they are the practices that support teachers in their instruction and students in their learning.

## The Role of the Principal

Learning environments influence the way children learn. Effective learning environments—to continue the argument—produce successful learners. Perhaps it is my bias because of my administrative experience, but I believe that, ultimately, it is the principal's responsibility to ensure and support effective learning environments in schools. In effect, principals set the tone for the entire school culture. That culture influences student behaviour, the degree of co-operation among staff, the nature of extracurricular activities, and the continuity of the learning experiences for the students. While principals can achieve this tone through a variety of administrative models—from autocratic to laissez-faire (Dreikurs, Grunwald, and Pepper 1982)—I have found that effective learning environments are those with democratic principals. These are schools where principals take part in all aspects of school life; where "the principal [might be found] play[ing] basketball with . . . [the] grade seven and eight boys who are working in a group for troubled readers" (Booth and Rowsell 2002, 44); where principals are as much a part of the school culture as they are its leaders; where principals share the responsibility of their authority with other teachers (Dreikurs, Grunwald, and Pepper 1982, 72).

Principals and school board administrators can achieve substantive school improvement by establishing professional learning communities. These communities are based on the following collaborative practices:

## Characteristics of Professional Learning Communities

◆ Work together to implement curriculum, instructional practices, and assessment.

◆ Work together to clarify intended learning outcomes.

◆ Develop common assessment practices and strategies.

◆ Jointly analyze student achievement data.

◆ Establish team improvement goals.

◆ Share learning strategies and materials.

◆ Engage in collective inquiry on student learning and apply research to teaching practices.

Figure 5.2

## Promoting Effective School Practices

Becoming an effective principal is not easy. It goes beyond just playing basketball with students. The position requires planning, soliciting staff support, and getting the community involved in the school. Teachers alone cannot be expected to coordinate these practices. Principals must help. (See Figure 5.3 on page 91.)

### Developing a Clear Mission Statement

Schools, like any organization, need to have an overall purpose or mission that guides their policies and helps set their

## Ten Practices That Create Effective Schools

Principals can help develop effective schools if they are able to facilitate with their teachers these practices:

1. Develop a clear mission statement.
2. Encourage high expectations.
3. Support instructional leadership practices.
4. Incorporate time-on-task practices.
5. Monitor student progress.
6. Provide a safe and orderly environment.
7. Encourage parent co-operation and involvement.
8. Participate in staff professional development.
9. Promote a multiplicity of teaching styles.
10. Reduce student alienation.

Figure 5.3

goals. Putting mission statements into words helps clarify them. If the statement makes little sense or is hard to follow, then it is likely that the ideas behind the statement are equally unclear.

So what constitutes a good mission statement? It reflects the expectations that *all* students can and will learn the school's essential curriculum. It does not exclude any group of students or presuppose that one cultural value is better than another. It is able to guide the principal and the school staff in making decisions about curriculum, instruction, assessment, student placement, and school activities.

> "The entire school leadership team, consisting of the principal, assistant administrators, and teacher-leaders, must share the commitment to all students being joyful, independent readers and writers" (Taylor and Collins 2003, 9).

## Encouraging High Expectations

Student success is directly related to a school climate of high expectations. Principals need to feel that the teaching staff can accomplish anything. Teachers need to assume that the students can learn anything. Students need to believe that they can achieve anything. I have witnessed how teacher expectations can make some students successful learners while causing others to become repeat failures. Research supports this observation: "Teachers appear to teach more and to teach it more warmly to students for whom they have more favorable expectations" (Rhem 1999). This conclusion is from the classic "Pygmalion in the Classroom" experiment conducted by Robert Rosenthal in the 1960s (Rosenthal and Jacobson 1992). Its methods and results are worth considering the next time an educator makes a snap judgment about a student.

For the experiment, a randomly selected group of students was chosen out of a larger population. "Teachers . . . were told that [selected students'] scores on the 'Test of Inflected Acquisition' indicated they would show surprising gains in intellectual competence during the next 8 months of school" (Rhem 1999). The test was actually a disguised, nonverbal intelligence test, and the scores for the selected group only represented a typical cross-section of students. At the end of the school year, when all the students in the study were again given the disguised intelligence test, the randomly selected students "showed a significantly greater gain than did the children of the control group. . . . The only difference between the experimental group and the control group children . . . was in the minds of the teachers" (ibid.).

Educators should feel responsible for the students' learning. They should be able to look beyond their learning difficulties to the strategies needed to overcome these deficiencies. And at the core of that responsibility should be the belief that all students *can* learn.

## Supporting Instructional Leadership Practices

Effective schools exhibit a leadership culture where every member of the teaching staff is a leader. Literacy advocates agree that "principals who share the responsibility of leadership are much more successful at creating positive change for teachers and students" (Booth and Rowsell 2002, 17). This shared leadership for principals, however, increases rather than reduces their responsibilities. In addition to their regular administrative duties, they need to become master teachers, team-teaching partners, school-support cheerleaders, and outreach program coordinators.

## Incorporating Time-On-Task Practices

Time (or more accurately, not enough time) continues to be a problem for school staffs. Curriculums are becoming more complex. Teachers are expected to teach more, and students are expected to learn more. In the past, when additional content was added to the curriculum, teachers knew what to do: *speed up*. Inevitably, those students who could not keep up were left out of the learning process. But effective schools reject this notion. All students need to have the opportunity to learn the core curriculum. While the school day cannot be lengthened—although I have conducted classes on Saturdays—school leaders can help teachers maximize their teaching time. This is particularly true for the principal. For example, principals can ensure that the essential curriculum is

"It is well documented that various schooling and testing practices discriminate (consciously or unconsciously) against various groups (e.g., against children from minority groups or lower socioeconomic levels). Children from various groups are also sometimes labeled as deficient because their home communication styles are not understood by teachers. . . . The same may certainly be true of many boys" (Smith and Wilhelm 2002, 4).

the primary focus for the school by

- minimizing interruptions to classroom instruction time.
- providing sufficient preparation time for teachers.
- promoting team planning sessions to support and guide teachers and support staff.
- helping develop accurate assessment tools.
- having sufficient materials and supplies available to all teachers.

## Monitoring Student Progress

If knowing one's students is important in teaching them, assessment is the key to understanding *how* to teach them. Assessment not only monitors student progress, but it informs teachers on what instructional methods to use. Principals need to schedule ample timetable periods for formative assessment (used by teachers during instruction) and out-of-class meetings (for teachers, students, and parents) where student work can be discussed.

It has been my practice as a principal to ask teachers to complete a basic assessment profile for every student by the end of September. This information is useful both as a beginning benchmark and as student background if discipline issues arise. Professional dialogues should be encouraged among teachers of consecutive grades throughout the school year. In this way, assessment data can be shared among the current and previous year's teachers. The focus of this assessment, of course, should always be on improving student learning, *not* on labelling student success or failure.

## Providing a Safe and Orderly Environment

The school environment reflects its students, staff and community. By the very nature of the institution—because schools deal with children—the issues of discipline and school rules play a major role in determining school cultures. As any beginning teacher soon comes to realize, teaching cannot take place with unruly students. The same can be said for the school as a whole: schools cannot be effective without a sense of order and stability. "Discipline . . . means teaching the child that there are certain rules in life that people live by" (Dreikurs, Grunwald, and Pepper 1982, 85).

However, maintaining a safe and orderly school environment can either be a negative or a positive process. Prohibitions are often necessary for children, but if a school relies only on its "do nots," its students will begin to feel imprisoned. Instead, the positive aspects of discipline need to be emphasized. Desirable behaviours, such as co-operation, should be recognized and reinforced. Students should be included in discussions about school rules and codes of conduct: "If we want our children to become thinking adults, the problem solving discussion [of discipline problems] not only teaches them fairness, it also teaches them to consider the alternative of various issues and situations" (ibid.).

## Encouraging Parent Co-operation and Involvement

When parents become involved in their children's learning, students are more likely to be successful in school. This is perhaps one of the greatest challenges that principals face: how to involve parents in the school culture. Teachers do their part on a class-by-class basis—sending letters home, conducting parent interviews, and seeking parent volunteers for class activities. Principals can help these endeavours by working to make the school a welcoming environment. (See pages 101–102 for a more detailed discussion on parental involvement.)

As noted previously, at-risk students often have parents who were themselves at-risk students. Change these parents' perceptions of what a school is and there is a good chance you will change their children's views as well.

## Participating in Staff Professional Development

Effective schools have staff development programs that focus on school improvement. Principals need to be part of the organizational team that coordinates these programs, as well as helping to initiate them. I have found that the year's first staff meeting is an excellent opportunity to begin the staff development process. By including in the agenda discussions on the school philosophy and the year's objectives, teachers can have the chance to offer their opinions and suggestions. This is also a good time to ask for ideas for professional development programs and to assemble coordinating committees if ones are not already active. Figure 5.4 below outlines some suggested questions that might be used as a focus for these early staff meetings.

Professional development sessions that answer these questions can assist staff to develop school improvement strategies.

### Where Have We Been? Where Are We Going?

- Does our school have a plan that clearly states our objectives?
- Does our school offer programs and services that best meet the needs of our students and community?
- Do our students achieve appropriate outcomes?
- Does our school participate in and initiate professional development activities?
- Does our school have assessment systems that enable us to accurately report on our students?
- Does our school use research-based knowledge to analyze its practices and assessment results?

Figure 5.4

## Promoting a Multiplicity of Teaching Styles

The challenge teachers face is how to recognize the variances among the students and how to offer these individuals instruction that matches their learning styles. This is an area where principals can greatly support their teachers by providing ongoing professional development in such areas as

- subject knowledge
- types of student learning styles
- a variety of instructional strategies

Principals should promote flexible teaching approaches to meet the needs of different students.

## Reducing Student Alienation

Students who are not performing up to the standard norm often feel alienated from the school culture. Student alienation can also occur in schools with large student populations or where students and teachers have few out-of-class relationships. Many of the above practices can help reduce this sense of alienation. Principals and teachers can further help by dividing large schools into smaller units. Within these divisions, students and staff will have more opportunities to meet and know each other. For example:

"Critical literacy, the practice of exploring and discussing the underlying assumptions in texts or works in other media, is a powerful tool for helping boys and girls "read" their world—for example, helping them become more aware of how various texts portray individuals, groups, and situations" (Ontario Ministry of Education 2004(b), 33).

- Co-operative learning environments offer students controlled opportunities to work with other students.
- Team-teaching activities introduce students to staff members other than their own teachers.

- Extracurricular school activities and clubs provide students with teacher-student experiences that are more informal than in-class relationships.
- Small groups and one-on-one teacher-student conferences encourage students to speak up and express their feelings.

## Racism and School Cultures

Effective schools are not only successful in creating good learning environments, they are also able to deal with the social and societal issues that affect their students. One such issue is how students approach cultural and ethnic diversity. Put children from different backgrounds together and the issues of racism and bigotry will most likely emerge. Although I do not believe that children are naturally prejudiced against people who are different from themselves, they can *learn* bias from friends, parents, and cultural groups.

While schools need a zero tolerance policy when it comes to racist and prejudiced behaviour, prohibition alone is not enough to curb it. Children need to understand how words and actions can harm people. One of the insidious elements of racism among school children is that if they do not speak out against it, they are, in effect, supporting it. The same holds true for a school's staff. If they do nothing to counter unacceptable behaviour, they are reinforcing it. Fortunately, there are many programs and practices schools have used that have been successful in reducing racism and intolerance. For example:

- developing school policies on race relations and intolerance
- promoting ongoing professional development discussions on racial and cultural issues
- organizing poster and essay contests that examine race relations

- reminding students to object to racist jokes and insults
- showing films and videos on prejudice, stereotyping, discrimination, and racism—followed by discussions
- examining the contents of the media for racist and stereotyping intent
- exploring ways in which community organizations and the school can work together to promote positive race and cultural relations
- inviting guests to speak on racism and human rights
- researching human-rights organizations in the community

Educators may not be able to change family and societal attitudes on racism, but they can insist that those views do not become part of the school culture.

## Parents and the School Environment

One morning when I was principal of an inner-city school, the mother of a former student came into the office. She presented me with a plaque in appreciation of the "outstanding and dedicated service" the staff had given her son and her family. We were all touched by the woman's gesture. It was what the staff had been working for in our school—to make these critical parent connections.

One of the most important factors affecting a child's performance in school is parental involvement (Ontario Ministry of Education 2004(b), 49). This is not always an easy task to

> "Parent support groups, advisory councils, and parent-teacher associations can support the quest for literacy through targeted fund-raisers, volunteer hours, tutoring hours, and the development of special events that support reading and writing" (Taylor and Collins 2003, 120).

accomplish. All too often, parents assume that sending their children to school and looking at their report cards is enough of a commitment. I cannot count the number of times at parents' nights that the only parents who turned up were those of students who were doing very well. Schools need to make parental involvement as important a goal as student achievement. In fact, they really cannot do otherwise, since the two are inseparable. I am sure that if the mother who presented us with the plaque had not thought so highly of the school and what we were trying to accomplish, her son would have not been so successful.

But how do schools get parents to become involved in their children's education? The first step is to get parents to work with their children at home.

## The Literacy Connection

Homework can seem as daunting to parents as it does to their children. Many of the topics in the current curriculum were not taught to children in generations past. This is especially true in mathematics and science. One area, however, where parents have proven to be effective co-teachers is in literacy. This is even true for immigrant families whose native language is not English. Consider the following activities that promote child literacy. Every parent should be able to do at least one of them.

- Read books and magazines to their children for thirty minutes every day; for non-English speaking families, read to them in their native language.
- Have books and magazines at home that their children can read.
- Make regular visits to the library with their children.

- Have books on tape (available at most libraries) for their children to listen to.

- Have family members make audio recordings of their children's favourite books.

- Ensure that there is free time set aside at home for reading.

- Read themselves, including books in their native language.

- Give children writing materials and encourage them to write about their experiences.

As well, teachers can encourage all of the above activities by sending letters home, talking to parents, and promoting the activities with the students. They can also develop take-home reading programs and provide students with appropriate reading lists. And, especially effective for boys, they can ask parents to keep reading logs of what their children read (Calkins 1996; McCarthy et al. 2001).

## Parents as Partners in Education

Principals can do their part to make these parent connections by making the school an inviting place for parents to visit. A parent reception area near the school office can welcome visitors with coffee and tea. Booklets about the school and its students can be displayed. Videos on the latest school activities and student accomplishments can be playing on a monitor. Perhaps an open-house barbecue might be held for staff, students, and parents as the parent letter on the next page describes.

"Our culture co-opts some of the most impressive qualities a boy can possess—their physical energy, boldness, curiosity, and action orientation—and distorts them into a punishing, dangerous definition of masculinity" (Kindlon and Thompson 2000, 15).

## Parent Letter Home

We hope that you had a restful and relaxing summer. The staff has spent many hours over the summer preparing for this coming school year. We recognize that our students' success will come from high expectations and basic codes of conduct. This cannot be accomplished without your help.

We look forward to seeing you at the Open House Barbecue on September __. At the barbecue, I will speak about our Parent Pact, which is outlined below. Your commitment to your child's learning will ensure his or her success.

### The Parent Pact

◆ I will try to make regular visits to the school and attend school events.

◆ I will regularly communicate with my child's teacher.

◆ I will daily monitor my child's schoolwork.

◆ I will make sure my child has a minimum of one hour of quiet time in the evening for school work.

◆ I will monitor the use of the telephone, television, and computer if they interfere with my child's homework.

◆ I will make sure that my child goes to bed and gets up at a reasonable time to ensure punctuality and school attentiveness.

Only through your co-operation and the commitment of staff and students can the above pact be accomplished.

Together we're better!

Sincerely,

Figure 5.5

Letters home are a good beginning, but in themselves they do not guarantee any real parent connections or commitments. As Linda Lambert advocates, schools need to see parents as partners, not as customers (2003, 67). The table that Lambert uses to compare traditional and ideal parental roles in schools is a good model to use to improve school and parent relationships (Figure 5.6).

If schools want to enhance their capacity to boost student learning—to become effective learning environments—they should work on building collaborative school cultures. Parents need to be an integral part of this collaboration.

## Parents as Partners

| Traditional Roles | Reciprocal Roles |
| --- | --- |
| Customers to be satisfied | Partners to be engaged |
| Servants of the school | Collaborators with staff |
| Obstacles to change | Facilitators of change |
| Critics to be persuaded | Co-learners |
| Instructional supporters | Co-teachers |
| Audience for staff decisions and actions | Decision makers with staff |
| Fund raisers | Resource developers |
| Clerks and helpers | Team members |

(Adapted from Lambert, 2003, 67)

Figure 5.6

## All-Boys Classrooms

Effective schools and parent involvement are essential if students are to be successful learners. But for many boys, the influence of the school is not enough. The disparity between the way girls and boys learn and behave can override all the efforts of teachers and parents. To overcome these hurdles, many schools in the United States and Canada are experimenting with all-boy classes. Indeed, researchers have found that boys in single-sex classrooms have greater self-confidence and are more willing to accept the idea that learning is for them (Sax 2002).

As studies have shown, boys of every age tend to be less enthusiastic about co-ed schools than girls (Gentry and Gable 2002). These findings appear to hold true for all types of school environments—urban and rural areas, affluent or low-income neighbourhoods. While single-sex classrooms are not the answer for all boys, school boards should consider setting up pilot programs.

For example, as Director of Education for the Hamilton Wentworth District School Board, I have observed the success of an all-boys class pilot project in one of our elementary schools, Cecil B. Stirling Elementary School. The teacher of the class has been pleased with the results: "I taught co-ed last year and I find this easier because you can find things that the whole group is interested in. It is easier for students to make an effort if they are interested in what they are doing. I try to draw on their prior knowledge and interests, which are usually sports related." Of course, for the teacher, there have been difficulties along the way: "My biggest challenges have been behaviour, respect, and concerns about their attitude toward literacy."

On the next page are some excerpts from a round-table discussion with the students and their parents from Hamilton's pilot all-boys class. Their comments not only offer insights into how the class has helped the boys' learning and school attitudes, but they support what researchers have discovered about male and female students.

## All-Boys Classes—Student Responses

| | |
|---|---|
| *Interviewer:* | *What do you like about the all-boys class?* |
| Matt: | A male teacher. They let you read magazines. |
| Doug: | It is hard to concentrate when you have a hot girl sitting in front of you. More motivating class challenges. |
| David: | The hockey tournament we had. Reports on movies instead of all these boring books. More focus on stuff that we like. |
| Stephen: | I have gotten better marks. I feel better about going to school. It is not so boring anymore. Our teacher talks about things instead of lecturing us. I feel better when asking questions in front of friends. |
| Jake: | In gym its better—a lot funnier stuff. . . . The teacher explains stuff. |
| Shae: | In English, we break everything up into shorter chunks. I ask dumb questions now and I am not scared to ask them. I am more motivated to do the work. We played hockey and then we wrote about it. |
| Josh: | Learning the same thing in a different way—something we can relate to. If we want to do well in school, we will. |

## All-Boys Classes—Parent Responses

| | |
|---|---|
| Valerie: | I have noticed a big change with his interest and attention span. He never says he is sick anymore and doesn't want to go to school. He can't wait to come home and share what he did. He is reading more at home. |
| Joan: | He's more focused. His marks have improved. The curriculum is geared toward him. The boys get rewarded. |
| Olivia: | I didn't want him in the class. I thought it would be a zoo. The right teacher is what is important. However, I am still concerned about French. |
| Grace: | It has been great. His marks have improved. He likes to act out a lot, but he gets to move around in this class. |
| Rick: | (Josh's father) It was Josh's choice. For him to read something at school and share with us at home is huge. He goes to the mailbox to get *Sports Illustrated*. |

# Works Cited

Allington, Richard L., and Sean A. Walmsley, eds. *No Quick Fix: Rethinking Literacy Programs in America's Elementary Schools.* New York: Teachers College Press; Newark, DE: International Reading Association, 1995.

Baron-Cohen, Simon. "They Just Can't Help It." *The Guardian,* 17 April 2003. Retrieved: 31 May 2005: http://www.guardian.co.uk/life/feature/story/0,13026,937913,00.html.

Bauer, Gabrielle. "Why Boys Must Be Boys: Is Your Son's School Giving Him What He Needs to Succeed?" Canada Online Edition: *Readers Digest.* Retrieved: 12 June 2002: http://readersdigestcalmag/2002/05/boys.html. First Published in *Canadian Living,* November 2001.

Beers, Kylene. *When Kids Can't Read: What Teachers Can Do, A Guide for Teachers 6–12.* Portsmouth, NH: Heinemann, 2003.

Bernard, Jean-Luc, David Hill, and Pat Falter. *Narrowing the Gender Gap: Attracting Men to Teaching.* Toronto: Ontario College of Teachers, 2004.

Biddulph, Steve. *Raising Boys: Why Boys Are Different—And How to Help Them Become Happy and Well-Balanced Men.* Berkeley, CA: Celestial Arts, 1997.

Blair, Heather and Kathy Sandford. "Canadian Adolescent Boys and Literacy," Edmonton: Department of Education University of Alberta and Victoria: Department of Education University of Victoria (2003). Retrieved 22 July 2005: http://www.education.ualberta.ca/boysandliteracy/findings.html.

Booth, David. *Even Hockey Players Read: Boys, Literacy and Learning.* Markham, ON: Pembroke, 2002.

Booth, David, and Jennifer Rowsell. *The Literacy Principal: Leading, Supporting and Assessing Reading and Writing Initiatives.* Markham, ON: Pembroke, 2002.

Brown, Louise. "Province strives to keep teens in school." *Toronto Star,* 18 May 2005, B1, B4.

Calkins, Lucy M. "Motivating Readers: First Things First: Planting the Seeds for Lifelong Reading." *Instructor,* 106(1) (August 1996): 32–33.

Canadian Education Statistics Council. *Education Indicators in Canada: Report of the Pan-Canadian Education Indicators Program 2003.* Toronto: Canadian Education Statistics Council, 2003.

Cassidy, Jane, and Karen Ditty. "Gender Differences Among Newborns on a Transient Otoacoustic Emissions Test for Hearing." *Journal of Music Therapy,* 38 (2001): 28–35.

Coles, Martin, and Christine Hall. "Gendered Readings: Learning from Childrens' Reading Choices." *Journal of Research in Reading,* 25 (1) (2002): 96–109.

Collins, Marva. *Ordinary Children, Extraordinary Teachers.* Charlottesville, VA: Hampton Roads Publishing, 1992.

Cone-Wesson, Barbara, and Glendy Ramirez. "Hearing sensitivity in newborns estimated from ABRs to bone-conducted sounds." *Journal of American Academy of Audiology,* 8 (1997): 299–307.

Correctional Services Canada. "Women in Prison: A Literature Review." Ottawa: Correctional Services Canada, 2002. Retrieved 14 October 2004: http://www.csc-scc.gc.ca/text/pblct/forum/e06/e061d_e.shtml.

Cox, Ruth E. "From *Boys' Life* to *Thrasher*: Boys and Magazines." *Teacher Librarian,* 30 (3) (February 2003): 25–26.

Doiron, Ray. "Boy Books, Girl Books: Should We Re-organize Our School Library Collections?" *Teacher Librarian,* 30 (3) (February 2003): 14–16.

Dreikurs, Rudolf, Bernice Bronia Grunwald, and Floy C. Pepper. *Maintaining Sanity in the Classroom: Classroom Management Techniques,* 2nd ed. New York: Harper and Row, 1982.

Dunne, Mary. *Education in Europe: Key statistics 2000/01.* Luxembourg: European Communities, 2003. Retrieved 5 October 2004: http://www.eds-destatis.de/en/downloads/sif/nk_03_13.pdf.

Edmonds, R. R. "Effective Schools for the Urban Poor." *Educational Leadership,* 37 (1979).

EQAO (Education Equality and Accountability Office) *Grade 3 and Grade 6 Assessment of Reading: Provincial Results: Detailed Data Tables.* Toronto: Education Equality and Accountability Office, 2004.

Gambell, Trevor, and Darryl Hunter. "Surveying Gender Differences in Canadian School Literacy." *Journal of Curriculum Studies,* 32 (5) (2000): 689–719.

Gentry, Marcia, and R. K. Gable. "Students' perceptions of classrooms activities: Are there grade level and gender differences?" *Journal of Educational Psychology,* 94 (2002): 539–544.

Gilroy, Kerri. "*Iron Man* Lesson Plan." Unpublished document, 2005.

Gurian, Michael. *A Fine Young Man: What Parents, Mentors and Educators Can Do to Shape Adolescent Boys into Exceptional Men.* New York: Putnam, 1998.

Gurian, Michael. *Boys and Girls Learn Differently: A Guide for Teachers and Parents.* San Francisco, CA: Jossey-Bass, 2001.

Gurian, Michael. *The Wonder of Boys: What Parents, Mentors and Educators Can Do to Shape Boys into Exceptional Men.* New York: Putnam, 1996.

Hamilton-Wentworth District School Board. *Literacy Guidelines Implementation Stages.* May 2003.

Heyman, Richard. *How to Say It to Boys: Communicating with Boys to Help Them Become the Best Men They Can Be.* New York: Prentice-Hall, 2003.

Haupt, Alison. "Where the Boys Are . . ." *Teacher Librarian,* 30 (3) (February 2003): 19–24.

Hyatt, Kay. "Reading Boys." *UMaine Today* (Online, 2002): 2(1), 12–13. Retrieved 12 June 2002 from http://www.umaine.edu/research/UMTReading.htm.

Jamieson, Brian. "Where Have All the Male Teachers Gone?" *Education Today,* 17 (1) (Spring 2005): 13–15.

Jobe, Ron, and Mary Dayton-Sakari. *Info-Kids: How to Use Nonfiction to Turn Reluctant Readers into Enthusiastic Learners.* Markham, ON: Pembroke, 2002.

Jones, Patrick, and Dawn Cartwright. "Overcoming the Obstacle Course: Teenage Boys and Reading." *Teacher Librarian,* 30 (3) (February 2003). Retrieved: 20 June 2005.

Kindlon, Dan, and Michael Thompson. *Raising Cain: Protecting the Emotional Life of Boys.* New York: Ballantine Books, 2000.

Kivel, Paul. *Boys Will Be Men: Raising Our Sons for Courage, Caring and Community.* Gabriola Island, BC: New Society Publishers, 1999.

Knowledge Loom, The. *Leadership for Literacy: High School Principals and the Reading Challenge.* Retrieved March 2002 from The Education Alliance at Brown University: The Knowledge Loom Website: http://www.principalspartnership.com.

Labinowicz, Ed. *The Piaget Primer: Thinking, Learning, Teaching.* Menlo Park, CA: Addison-Wesley, 1980.

Ladson-Billings, Gloria. "Toward a Theory of Culturally Relevant Pedagogy." *American Education Research Journal,* 35 (1995): 465–491.

Lambert, Linda. *Leadership Capacity for Lasting School Improvement.* Alexandria, VA: Association for Supervision and Curriculum Development, 2003.

Lewis, Maureen, and David Wray. *Extending Literacy: Developing Approaches to Non-fiction.* London: Taylor & Francis, 1997.

McCarthy, S., J. Nicastro, I. Spiros, and K. Staley. "Increasing Recreational Reading Through the Use of Read-Alouds." Unpublished manuscript. Chicago, IL: Saint Xavier University, 2001.

McKeachie, W. J. "Learning Styles Can Become Learning Strategies." *The National Teaching and Learning Forum,* 4 (6) (November 1995). Retrieved: 19 June 2005: http://www.ntlf.com/html/pi/9511/article1.htm.

McMahon, S., T. Raphael, V. Goatley, & L. Pardo., eds. *The Book Club Connection: Literacy, Learning and Classroom Talk.* Englewood, CO: Teachers College Press, 1997.

Millard, Elaine. *Differently Literate: Boys, Girls and the Schooling of Literacy.* Washington, DC: Falmer Press, 1997.

Mind Tools Ltd. *Mind Tools.* Retrieved 10 January 1999: http://www.mindtools.com/mnemlsty.html.

Mitchell, Alanna. "Goodbye, Mr. Chips." Toronto: *The Globe and Mail.* 17 January 2004, F1.

Morrow, Lesley Mandel, and Ellen M. O'Connor. "Literacy Partnerships for Change with 'High Risk' Kindergartens." In *No Quick Fix: Rethinking Literacy Programs in America's Elementary Schools*

(97–115). New York: Teachers College Press; Newark, DE: International Reading Association, 1995.

Noble, Colin, and Wendy Bradford. *Getting It Right for Boys . . . and Girls.* London: Routledge, 2000.

Norris, Doreen, and Joyce Boucher. *Observing Children Through Their Formative Years.* Toronto: The Board of Education for the City of Toronto, 1980.

Ontario College of Teachers. *Narrowing the Gender Gap: Attracting Men to Teaching.* Toronto: Ontario College of Teachers, November 2004.

Ontario Ministry of Education. *Early Reading Strategy: the Report of the Expert Panel on Early Reading in Ontario.* Toronto: Ontario Ministry of Education, 2003(a).

Ontario Ministry of Education. *Guide to Effective Instruction in Reading: Kindergarten to Grade 3.* Toronto: Ontario Ministry of Education, 2003(b).

Ontario Ministry of Education. *Think Literacy Success: The Report of the Expert Panel on Students at Risk in Ontario.* Toronto: Ontario Ministry of Education, 2003(c).

Ontario Ministry of Education. *Literacy for Learning: the Report of the Expert Panel on Literacy in Grades 4 to 6 in Ontario.* Toronto: Ontario Ministry of Education, 2004(a).

Ontario Ministry of Education. *Me Read? No Way! A Practical Guide to Improving Boys' Literacy Skills.* Toronto: Ontario Ministry of Education, 2004(b).

Piaget, Jean. *The Grasp of Consciousness: Action and Concept in the Young Child.* Translated by Susan Wedgewood. Cambridge, MA: Harvard University Press, 1976.

Pollack, William. *Real Boys: Rescuing Our Sons from the Myths of Boyhood.* New York: Henry Holt and Company, 1998.

Raphael, T. "The Book Club Plus Network: What counts as teacher research?" *Language Arts,* 77 (1) (1999): 48–52.

Raphael, T., S. Florio-Ruane, and M. George. "Book Club Plus: A Conceptual Framework to Organize Literacy Instruction." *Language Arts,* 79 (2) (2001): 159–169.

Rhem, James. "Pygmalion in the Classroom." *The National Teaching and Learning Forum,* 8 (2) (February 1999). Retrieved: 19 June 2005: http://www.ntlf.com/html/pi/9902/pygm_1.htm.

Rosenthal, Robert, and Lenore Jacobson. *Pygmalion in the Classroom.* New York: Rinehart and Winston, 1968. Later edition: Rosenthal, Robert, and Lenore Jacobson. *Pygmalion in the Classroom: Teacher Expectation and Pupils' Intellectual Development.* New York: Irvington Publishers, 1992.

Sax, Leonard. "Single-Sex Education: Ready for Prime-time?" *The World and I* (2001). Retrieved: 1 August 2002: http://www.singlesexschools.org/worldandi.html.

Sax, Leonard. *Why Gender Matters: What Parents and Teachers Need to Know About the Emerging Science of Sex Differences.* New York: Doubleday, 2005.

Scieszka, Jon. "Why Johnny Won't Read" Washington, DC: *Washington Post,* 2 June 2002, BW06.

Scieszka, Jon. "Guys and Reading." *Teacher Librarian,* 30:3 (February 2003): 17–18.

Shaw, George Bernard. *Back to Methuselah,* Part I, Act I. London: Constable, 1921.

Silverstein, Olga, and Beth Rashbaum. *The Courage to Raise Good Men.* New York: Penguin, 1994.

Simpson, Anne. "Fictions and Facts: An Investigation of the Reading Practices of Girls and Boys." *English Education,* 28 (4) (December 1996): 268–279.

Smith, Michael W., and Jeffrey D. Wilhelm. *Reading Don't Fix No Chevys: Literacy in the Lives of Young Men.* Portsmouth, NH: Heinemann, 2002.

Sommers, Christina Hoff. *The War Against Boys: How Misguided Feminism Is Harming Our Young Men.* New York: Simon and Schuster, 2000.

Sommers, Christina Hoff. "Boys and Their Mothers." *The Atlantic Online.* Retrieved: May 2000: http://www.theatlantic.com/issues/2005/05/sommers4.htm.

Spence, Christopher M. *On Time! On Task! On a Mission!: A Year in the Life of a Middle School Principal.* Halifax, NS: Fernwood Publishing, 2002.

Statistics Canada. "Family Violence." Ottawa: Statistics Canada, 2003. Retrieved: 23 June 2003: http://www.statcan.ca/Daily/English/030623/d030623c.htm.

Steel, C. M. "Race and the Schooling of Black Americans." *Atlantic Monthly,* 26 (4) (1992).

Strickland, Dorothy S., Kathy Ganske, and Joanne K. Monroe. *Supporting Struggling Readers and Writers: Strategies for Classroom Intervention 3–6.* Portland, ME: Stenhouse Publishing; Newark, DE: International Reading Association, 2002.

Taylor, Rosemarye, and Valerie Doyle Collins. *Literacy Leadership for Grades 5–12.* Alexandria, VA: Association for Supervision and Curriculum Development, 2003.

Walp, Trudy P., and Sean A. Walmsley, "Scoring Well on Tests or Becoming Genuinely Literate: Rethinking Remediation in a Small Rural School" in *No Quick Fix: Rethinking Literacy Programs in America's Elementary Schools* (177–196). New York: Teachers College Press, 1995.

Wilson, John. "How to Get Boys Reading." *Quill & Quire* (April 2005): 11.

Young, Josephine Peyton, and William G. Brozo. "Boys Will Be Boys, or Will They?: Literacy and Masculinities." *Reading Research Quarterly,* 36 (3) (2001): 316–325.

# Index

learning: communities, 90; environments, 89; as social activity, 73

learning, styles of: active versus visual, 46; auditory, 50; gender differences in, 46, 104; kinesthetic, 50; visual, 50

lessons: model for boys, 47–48; planning for boy learners, 46–47

listening to boys, 44–45, 83

literacy: connections, 21; culturally relevant approach to, 73; family and societal influences, 13; gender differences in, 12, 24, 104; leadership in, 86–90; parent connection, 100–101; and professional development, 67; roadblocks to, 27–28; school-wide, 67

literacy outreach programs, 65–70. *See also* outreach programs.

males: stereotypical behaviour of, 56–57; and teaching, 25, 26

mentors and mentoring, 61; in Boys to Men, 74, 75, 76, 81, 82, 83; in Project Pride, 72; as role models, 58, 76

outreach programs, 62–64, 68–70, 86; bottom line for, 82–83; characteristics of, 69–70; literacy, *see* literacy outreach programs; mentoring in, 76, 81; strategic plan for, 64. *See also* book clubs; Boys to Men; Project Pride; Read to Succeed.

parents: of at-risk students, 95–96; and Boys to Men program, 82; and homework, 100; involvement in school, 95, 99–100; and the parent pact, 102; as partners in education, 101–103; principals and, 95, 101; promotion of child literacy, 100–101; school environment and, 99–103

peers: relationships, 55; support of, 28; work with, 41

principals: and leadership, 89–90, 93; and parents, 95, 101; and professional development, 96; and staff meetings, 96

problem solving, 14, 24–25

professional development, 28, 67, 96

professional learning communities, 90

Project Pride, 70–72

racism, 98–99

reading: aloud, 55, 57; boys' opinion of, 45–51; boys' versus girls', 18–20; buddy program, 28, 58; choices for boys, 18–20, 44–45, 46, 67; culture of, 54; as a female activity, 20; real-world connections to, 21; role models for, 20–21, 55; supporting, 54–57; and writing, 57–58

Read to Succeed, 72–73

research-based knowledge, 26, 29–31, 46–47; analyzing, 32; data collection, 30, 31–32; evaluation, 30; intervention, 30; re-assessment, 30

research-based knowledge, model for: cognitive development, 36–38; conclusion, 42–43; physical development, 38–39; pre-assessment, 34–35; record sheet, 34; social/emotional, 40–41

role models, 60, 74, 75, 76

schools: behaviour in, 95; and book clubs, *see* book clubs; effective practices in, *see* effective school practices; environment, 94–95; graduation from, 25–26; literacy in, 67; and social change, 27; student data collection in, 31–32; as waste of time, 27

self-esteem, 71, 77

struggling readers, 11–12

students: alienation of, 97–98; assessment of, 94; knowledge of, 29–31

subjects, hard versus soft, 23–24

teachers: changing demographics of, 25–27; female, 20, 25, 26; male, 25, 26; professional dialogues among, 55; reading aloud, 55; as role models, 55

teaching, styles of, 97

thought books, 42–43

vision, 16–17

writing, reading and, 57–58